Study

Marine Science
The Dynamic Ocean

Meghan E. Marrero, Ed.D.
Glen Schuster, M.S.

Print Components

Student Edition
Teacher's Edition
Study Workbook

Technology Components

Marine Science website: www.us-satellite.net/marinescience
Classroom Resources: "e-Tools" DVD ROM
Signals of Spring website: www.signalsofspring.net
Examview® CD-ROM

Copyright © 2012 U.S. Satellite Laboratory, Inc. All Rights Reserved. Printed in the United States of America. This publication is protected by copyright, and permission should be obtained from the publisher prior to any prohibited reproduction, storage in a retrieval system, or transmission in any form or by any other means, electronic, mechanical, photocopying, recording, or likewise. For information regarding permissions, write to U.S. Satellite Laboratory, Inc., 32 Elm Place, Rye, New York 10580.

Pearson®, Prentice Hall®, and Pearson Prentice Hall® are trademarks, in the U.S. and/or other countries, of Pearson Education, Inc., or its affiliates.

Use of the trademarks or company names implies no relationship, sponsorship, endorsement, sale, or promotion on the part of U.S. Satellite Laboratory, Inc.

U.S. Satellite
Laboratory

ISBN-13: 978-0-13-319218-6

10 19

Contents

1 Diving Into Ocean Ecosystems 1

2 Water on Earth 11

3 More About Water 23

4 The Ocean Over Time 37

5 Migrations in the Sea 47

6 Explore the Seafloor 59

7 The Formation of the Ocean 69

8 Seasons of Change 79

9 The Sea Surface: The Great Energy Distributor 87

10 Energy and the Ocean 99

11 Weather, Climate, and the Ocean 109

12 Voyage to the Deep 117

13 Photosynthesis in the Ocean 131

14 Biodiversity in the Ocean 145

15 Marine Populations 157

16 Population Changes 169

17 Food Webs in Action 181

18 Introduction to Marine Invertebrates 191

19 Biology of Fishes 205

20 Marine Reptiles and Birds 219

21 Marine Mammals 231

22 Relationships in the Sea 247

23 The Ocean's Waves 257

24 A Time for Tides 267

25 Animal Needs and Animal Tracking 277

26 Student Expert Research 287

27 Student Expert Analysis 297

28 Which Way to the Sea? 307

29 Nonpoint Source Pollution 317

30 Point Source Pollution 331

31 Humans and Coastlines 345

32 The Ocean's Resources 353

33 Changing Climate 363

34 Protecting Marine Habitats 373

Diving Into Ocean Ecosystems

BIGIDEAS

- An ecosystem is the interactions of all the living and non-living things in an environment, including its energy source.

- Biotic factors are all the living organisms in an ecosystem, while abiotic factors are all the non-living things in an ecosystem.

- Succession is a process of gradual changes that occur naturally in an environment. During this process living organisms replace other living organisms until a stable community is reached.

Engage

Activate Prior Knowledge

Throughout your study of *Marine Science: The Dynamic Ocean*, you will explore Earth's ocean and uncover many of its mysteries. Although there is much to learn, it is likely that you already know about and have had experiences with the ocean and ocean organisms. You may have swum in the ocean on a warm day. You may have visited an aquarium filled with ocean creatures. You may have eaten fish or purchased other products that came from the ocean.

Write about an experience you have had that involves the ocean in some way.

_____

_____

_____

_____

_____

_____

_____

Reading Strategy: TAKING NOTES

Taking notes when you read is an important tool that can help you remember key concepts. One way to take notes and keep new information organized is by using a concept web such as the one below. A concept web is a type of graphic organizer used to show ideas that are related to a topic or concept. Concept webs can help you show relationships between ideas.

The Engage section of your textbook introduces you to scientific inquiry—the process you will use as a scientist to investigate the migration patterns of marine animals. As you read Page 4 of the textbook, use the concept web to record key ideas about the work of scientists. Then, use this note-taking skill as you complete other sections of the Lesson.

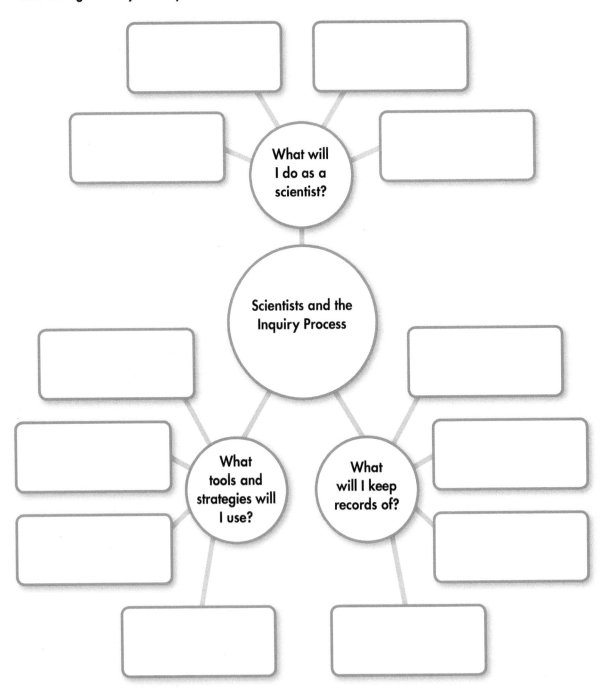

Visual Literacy: Reading Maps

Reading and interpreting maps will be an important part of your journey in this Marine Science course. You will study maps as you track a marine animal species across the globe and will be expected to explain where on the map your animal is and where it is likely to move. In addition, you will analyze maps as you learn about ocean environments, currents, and conditions of the ocean.

Before reading and trying the activities in your textbook, review the world map below. Label the oceans and continents. Then, answer the Questions that follow.

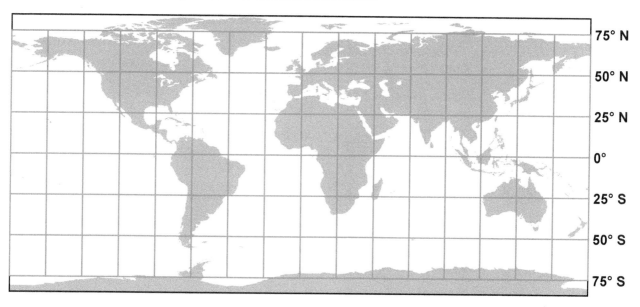

1. Which continents touch the Atlantic Ocean? _____

   _____

2. Which continents touch the Indian Ocean? _____

   _____

3. Where does one ocean stop and another start? Are the oceans separate bodies of water,

   or one continuous body? _____

   _____

4. Predict which covers more of Earth—water or land? _____

   _____

You can make an estimate of how much of Earth's surface is covered by land and how much is covered by ocean. Do this by using a map with a grid. On Page 3, the map's projection makes Earth's Polar Regions appear to be bigger than they are, so using this map, consider only the square units between 75° S to 75° N when doing this exercise.

Now calculate how much of Earth is covered by land and how much is covered by ocean. Using the blue grid on the world map, count how many squares are more "filled" by land and how many by water. Consider "filled" as greater than 50%. Then, follow the steps below to calculate the percentage of land mass covering Earth's surface and the percentage of ocean mass. You may be surprised at the answer.

Count and record the number of boxes each for:

Land = _____ squares

Ocean = _____ squares

Total number of squares = _____

Percentage of land:

Divide the number of squares for land by the total number of squares.

_____ ÷ _____ = _____

Multiply the number that you calculated above by 100 to calculate an estimate for percentage of land.

_____ × 100 = _____ %

Percentage of ocean:

Divide the number of squares for ocean by the total number of squares.

_____ ÷ _____ = _____

Multiply the number that you calculated above by 100 to calculate an estimate for percentage of ocean.

_____ × 100 = _____ %

5. Which covers more of Earth's surface—land or ocean? _____

Explore

Build Background

The activity on Pages 6–7 of your textbook asks you to explore marine ecosystems. An ecosystem is the interaction of all the living and non-living things in an area, including its energy source. The living things, such as the plants and animals, make up the biotic factors. The non-living things, such as water, soil, air, and sunlight, make up the abiotic factors. Living things in an ecosystem depend on the abiotic factors of their ecosystem and on one another for their survival.

Before trying the activity in your textbook, use the chart below to list all the biotic and abiotic factors in your "classroom ecosystem" to familiarize yourself with these concepts. Then, answer the Questions that follow.

Biotic factors	Abiotic factors
Example: class pet	Example: desk

1. Did you find more biotic or abiotic factors in your classroom ecosystem? _____

   _____

2. How do the biotic factors depend on one another and on the abiotic factors of the

   ecosystem? _____

   _____

3. How is your classroom ecosystem similar to your school ecosystem? How does it differ?

   _____

   _____

Explain

Review What You Learned

The list of marine ecosystems and their descriptions below are out of order. Match the ecosystem in the first column to the appropriate description of its characteristics in the second column. Record the letter of the correct description on the line provided.

Marine Ecosystems

Descriptions

1. _____ The Open Ocean

   a. Environment with strong wave action; organisms are adapted to both wet and dry conditions

2. _____ Coral Reef

   b. Wet and dry environment; long grasses; thick mud

3. _____ Kelp Forest

   c. Extremely cold environment dominated by ice; very little sunlight during parts of the year

4. _____ Mangrove Forest

   d. Sunny environment with dense forest of fast-growing seaweed

5. _____ Rocky Shore

   e. Environment far from landforms with plenty of light and water temperatures that vary with depth; marine organisms can move about freely

6. _____ Polar Sea

   f. Dark environment with cold water temperature; few animal communities

7. _____ Salt Marsh

   g. Environment with warm temperatures; tree roots are covered during high tide and exposed during low tide

8. _____ Deep Ocean

   h. Warm and shallow environment; built from seafloor; rich diversity of marine life

Elaborate

Vocabulary Review

Complete the chart below as you read Pages 9–15 of your textbook. Write the definition of each vocabulary term in your own words. Then, write a note to yourself on how you will remember the meaning of each term. Use the chart to review key concepts after you have finished the Lesson.

Term	Definition	How I Will Remember
Biological community		
Ecosystem		
Organism		
Succession		
Benthic		
Mangrove		

Reading Strategy: SEQUENCE of EVENTS

Pages 9–12 of your textbook describe whale falls and how a whale carcass is slowly consumed and broken down by communities of marine organisms. Keeping track of the sequence in which processes such as this occur can help you understand processes and changes that happen over time. Remember, a sequence describes the order in which something happens.

After reading Pages 9–12 of your textbook, use the Sequence of Events graphic organizer below to record in your own words the major stages in which a whale carcass is broken down.

Evaluate

Lesson Summary

- The work of scientists includes asking questions, making observations, drawing conclusions, and keeping detailed notes of research and experiments.

- Scientists use a variety of tools and technologies to observe and learn about an animal's movements and behavior.

- The ocean covers more than 70% of Earth and includes many diverse ecosystems.

- An ecosystem is made up of the interactions of all the living organisms (biotic factors) and non-living things (abiotic factors) in an area along with its energy source—typically the Sun.

- The relationship between organisms and their physical environment is important to the health of an ecosystem and the life that can exist.

- Succession is the process in which communities found in an ecosystem change over time. One species may increase its population, while another species may disappear. The replacement of one population by another occurs until a stable community is formed.

- Succession may be triggered in an ecosystem by gradual changes such as the death and decay of one or a small group of organisms to drastic changes such as tropical storms or oil spills that affect entire populations at once.

- Whale falls feed communities of marine organisms and provide an example of succession.

- National Marine Sanctuaries are a system of 14 marine protected areas in the United States. These National Marine Sanctuaries were created to protect marine habitats and organisms.

Lesson Review

Complete the crossword puzzle on the next page to review key terms and concepts from the Lesson.

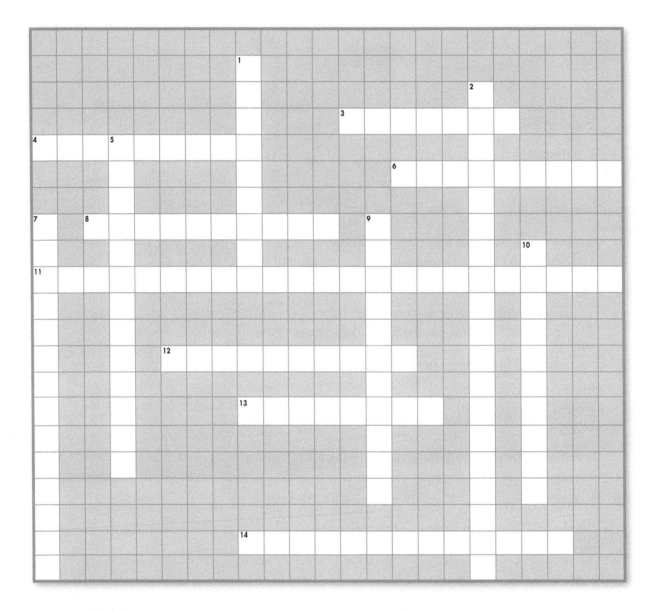

ACROSS

3. Related to the bottom of the ocean
4. Living things
6. Dead whale that settles onto the ocean floor
8. Organisms that eat bones
11. Federally protected coastal marine environment
12. What happens to a dead whale over years
13. A tropical tree that grows in salt water
14. Living parts of an ecosystem

DOWN

1. The living and non-living things interacting in an environment
2. All the organisms living together in an environment
5. A non-living part of an ecosystem
7. Lives on the whale skeleton
9. Types of marine organism on a whale carcass
10. Changes in an ecological community that occur over time

2 Water on Earth

BIG IDEAS

- Nearly three-quarters of Earth is covered by water, the majority of which is salt water found in the ocean.

- Water has many unique properties that shape our planet and life on Earth.

- All living things depend on water for survival.

Engage

Activate Prior Knowledge

In this Lesson you will learn about the unique properties of water and how these properties influence Earth and life on our planet. Before reading and trying the activities in your textbook, use the chart below to record what you already know about these topics. After you complete the Lesson, use the chart to record new information you learned.

Read each Question below and think about what you already know about the topic. Write a few ideas, thoughts, or sentences in the What I Know column of the chart.

Question	What I Know	What I Learned
What are some properties of water?		
Where does water exist as a solid and why is this important?		
What does it mean to be a renewable resource? What are some nonrenewable resources?		
Why is water important to both marine organisms and humans?		

Explore

Vocabulary Review

Using Pages 22–26 of your textbook, complete the activities below to review key vocabulary. For Questions 1–5, match each lab material to its correct definition.

1. _____ Tap water

    a. Solid carbon dioxide commonly used to keep foods cold during shipping

2. _____ Dry ice

    b. Water in the solid state

3. _____ Salt water

    c. Pure water with all substances removed

4. _____ Ice

    d. Fresh water from a faucet, which has been treated to kill bacteria and harmful substances

5. _____ Distilled water

    e. Water that contains dissolved salts

For Questions 6–11, draw a line to match each term to its correct description.

6. Sublimation   The temperature at which a liquid begins to change into a solid

7. Freezing point   The temperature at which a liquid begins to change into a gas

8. Melting point   The temperature at which a solid begins to change into a liquid

9. Boiling point   The process of changing from a solid to a gas

10. Density   The attraction between molecules at a liquid's surface

11. Surface tension   The amount of mass in a given volume of a substance

Use the Explore section of your text to answer the Questions below.

12. What three forms does water exist in on Earth? _____

_____

13. What is a hypothesis? _____

_____

_____

14. Why is dry ice dangerous to touch? _____

Practice Process Skills: DEFINING VARIABLES

When conducting an investigation, we often observe or make measurements of things that change. These are variables. Keeping track of variables in an experiment is important because it helps you analyze and understand your results. Remember from the experiment your class conducted in Lesson 2, there are two major types of variables. An **independent variable** is not affected by the other variables in an experiment. It is often something that a scientist changes in order to do an experiment. Experiments should have only one independent variable. A **dependent variable** depends on other factors in the experiment. It is often the thing we are trying to learn more about and is the experimental results. A third type of variable is a **controlled variable**. This is what a scientist keeps similar in all parts of the experiment. There are often multiple controlled variables. Scientists try to make sure that controlled variables do not affect the outcome or results of an experiment.

In the Explore section of your text, you conducted several experiments on the phase changes of water.

1. What was the *independent variable* in these experiments? _____

_____

2. What was the *dependent variable*? _____

_____

3. What were the *controlled variables*, or the things you tried to keep the same in each part

of the experiments? _____

_____

_____

_____

Now that we have learned what variables are, try to identify each variable in the experiments below.

A group of first grade students planted seeds in cups of soil. They placed some cups near the windows to get sunlight and others in a closet where no light was present. After a week, they measured the growth of the plants.

4. What is the *independent variable* in this experiment? _____

5. What is the *dependent variable*? _____

6. What are some of the *controlled variables*? _____

_____

_____

A group of high school students wanted to use a decibel meter to test whether or not their classroom was noisier when their science teacher left the room.

7. What is the *independent variable* in this experiment? _____

8. What is the *dependent variable*? _____

9. What are some of the *controlled variables*? _____

_____

_____

Explain

Complete the chart below as you read Pages 26–29 of your textbook. Write the definition of each vocabulary term in your own words. Then, write a note or draw a picture to help you remember the meaning of each term. Use the chart to review key concepts after you have finished the Lesson.

Term	Definition	Example/Model/Drawing
Atom		
Valence electron		
Molecule		
Covalent bond		
Polar covalent bond		

Term	Definition	Example/Model/Drawing
Polar covalent molecule		
Hydrogen bonding		

Review What You Learned

After reading Pages 26–29 of your textbook, answer the Questions below to review what you learned.

1. What kind of charge does each atomic particle have?

   Neutron _____

   Proton _____

   Electron _____

2. How many atoms make up a water molecule? What are they?

   _____

   _____

   _____

3. What kind of molecule is water? Explain what this means in your own words.

    _____

    _____

    _____

4. Make a diagram of a water molecule. Label the atoms and show the electric charge associated with each.

5. Water's molecular structure gives it certain properties. What are some of these special properties?

    _____

    _____

    _____

Visual Literacy: Reading Graphs

Pages 30–31 of your textbook discuss phase changes and show a graph called a phase change diagram. Graphs, maps, and charts are often used in science to show information in a visual way. They are as important as the text you read. Knowing how to read and understand information from graphs and other images is an important skill.

Below is a phase change diagram. As heat is added to a material, the material gains energy and its temperature rises. If enough energy is gained, its state changes. Use Pages 30–31 in your text to help you answer the Questions below and review how to read and interpret graphs.

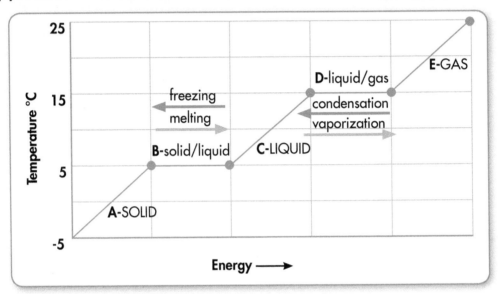

1. What is the freezing temperature of this substance? _____

2. What letter represents the melting point of the substance? _____

3. What is the boiling temperature of the substance? _____

4. What happens as the solid changes to a liquid? _____

5. What is vaporization? How is it shown on the diagram? _____

   _____

6. What is freezing? How is it shown on the diagram? _____

   _____

Elaborate

Practice Process Skills: RECORDING DATA

During scientific investigations, we make observations and collect data. Data is factual information. Your name and height are data about you. Carefully recording data is a key part of scientific research. Detailed notes help us review our work and help us to analyze and draw conclusions about our results.

Scientists often use data tables to record information in a quick and organized way. In a data table, information is arranged in labeled rows and columns. Data tables can help you find information at a glance. They can also be helpful in interpreting information that either you, or others, have gathered. It is always useful to know what kind of data you will collect and need to record before starting an investigation. This way you'll be sure to keep careful notes.

Throughout the investigations on Pages 32–33 of your textbook you will record data in tables. Before trying the activities, skim through the procedures. Then, answer the following Questions.

1. What data will you record in the *Floating and Sinking* experiment? _____

   _____

   _____

   _____

2. Look at the data table you will complete in *Floating and Sinking*.

   What information will you record in column 1? _____

   What information will you record in column 5? _____

3. How will recording your predictions, observations, and calculations in a data table help

   you interpret and compare your results? _____

   _____

   _____

   _____

Math Mini-Lesson

For the *Floating and Sinking* activity on Pages 32–33 of your textbook, you will calculate the density of various items. Density is defined as a material's mass per unit volume. You can think of density as how compact something is. When a lot of mass is packed in a small space, density is high. When little mass is packed in a large space, density is low.

Before trying the activity in your textbook, use the formula below to practice calculating density.

$$\text{Density} = \frac{\text{mass}}{\text{volume}}$$

To calculate density we divide an object's mass by its volume. Here's an example. Suppose a piece of wood has a mass of 5.85 g and a volume of 7.57 cm³. Its density would be:

$$\frac{5.85 \text{ g}}{7.57 \text{ cm}^3} = 0.773 \text{ g/cm}^3$$

1. Cooking oil has a mass of 22.75 g and a volume of 25 mL. What is its density? Show your work.

2. A piece of lead has a mass of 170 g and a volume of 15 cm³. What is its density? Show your work.

3. A helium balloon has a mass of 0.036 g and a density of 0.00018 g/cm³. What is the volume? Show your work.

Name _____ Class _____ Date _____

You have now learned about the property of density and how it affects marine organisms. Use Pages 34–37 in your text to complete the chart below.

DENSITY

↓

What is it? (Definition)

What is the average density of?

Salt water:

Fresh water:

Define these terms associated with density:

Neutral Buoyancy:

Sea Ice:

How does the property of density affect marine organisms? (give at least 3 examples)

Evaluate

Lesson Summary

- Most of the planet's surface is covered by water. Ninety-seven percent of this water is salt water found in the planet's oceans. The remaining three percent of water on Earth is fresh water.

- Water has many unique properties that shape life on Earth.

- Water on Earth exists in all three states of matter—solid, liquid, and gas.

- All living things depend on water for survival.

- Marine organisms use and depend on the ocean's properties to meet their needs. Properties include density and the ocean's ability to change into different states of matter.

- Water is considered a renewable resource. However, we must treat it with respect to ensure that the resources within the water are there for future generations

When you have completed the Lesson, turn back to Page 11 of this workbook and record information you gained from the Lesson in the What I Learned column of the chart.

3 More About Water

BIG IDEAS

- Cohesion and surface tension are two of water's many unique properties.

- Many things, such as salt, dissolve in water.

- The ocean's salinity directly affects how marine organisms function.

- All of these factors play a role in how marine animals must adapt to their environment.

Engage

Activate Prior Knowledge

Below is an anticipation guide. It includes statements related to what you will read in this Lesson. Some of the statements are accurate, while others are not. Completing an anticipation guide before you read can help you recall information you know about a topic and get you prepared for reading. When you have finished the Lesson, you will review your responses and compare them with what you have learned.

Before reading the Lesson, review each statement in the chart and record whether you agree or disagree with the statement. Use what you have learned in the previous Lessons to help you make your decisions. After you have read the Lesson, you will return to the guide to correct your statements.

Statement	Agree/Disagree	Explanation
Metals are one of the components of salt.		
Most of the salt in the ocean comes from decaying organisms.		

Name _____ Class _____ Date _____

Statement	Agree/Disagree	Explanation
Many materials can dissolve in water.		
Marine organisms require fresh water to live.		
The salt content of the ocean varies a lot from one place to another.		
Marine mammals drink seawater.		
The attraction of water molecules between each other is weak.		
Many animals rely on the property of cohesion in order to feed and release waste.		
Salt water has the ability to conduct electricity.		

Explore

Vocabulary Review

Complete the paragraph below with the missing terms from the word bank below. Use Page 43 in your text to help you.

solvent	solution	saturated	solute	solubility

Water is referred to as a _____ because many substances dissolve in it. During an experiment in class, you added salt to beakers of water in order to test its _____, or to see how well it dissolved in a solvent. The salt in this experiment is referred to as a _____ because you are testing how it dissolves in a solvent. When you mixed the water and salt together, you made what is called a _____, a mixture of two substances. At some point, you were unable to add any more salt to the water. This is because the solution became _____ and was unable to dissolve any more solute.

Concept Review

In the Explore section of the text, you are asked to conduct a lab to test solubility. Use Pages 43 through 45 of your text to help you answer the Questions below.

1. You are directed to use the same volume of water for each part of the lab. Why do you think you need to record the volume if it always remains the same? _____

    _____

    _____

2. Why do you think you need to record the starting mass of the salt? _____

    _____

    _____

3. What is a **dependent variable**? What is the dependent variable in this experiment? _____

    _____

    _____

    _____

4. As the temperature of the water increases, what happens to the solubility? What does this

    mean? _____

    _____

Math Mini-Lesson

In the Explore section of Lesson 3, you are asked to create a **line graph**. On a line graph, each variable is plotted along an **axis**. A graph has a vertical, or y-axis, and a horizontal, or x-axis. Each of these axes must be labeled with the information that is being graphed. Your final product should also be titled. A **scale** across the horizontal and the vertical axes tells how much, how many, or years, days, etc. of what you are plotting. If the data is measured in months, years, or days, the scale is already created for you. However, if your data is measured in numbers, creating a scale can be tricky. Most scales start with 0 on the bottom of the y axis, unless the lowest number is much higher than that. The scale must include all numbers represented in your data, and often goes one number, or interval above the highest number in your data. The **interval** separates the scale into equal parts. Intervals may be counted by 1s, 5s, 10s, etc. depending on what data you are using. The **points** on the graph show us where your data from the x and y axes intersect. On a line graph, the last step is to connect the points with a **line** to complete the line graph. Line graphs help to show trends in data over time and enable those interpreting the graph to make predictions about data that has not yet been graphed.

Below is a sample line graph. Use the graph to help you answer the Questions that follow. You are then provided with data to create your own line graph.

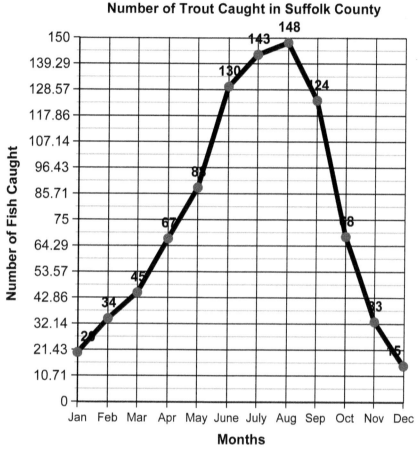

Number of Trout Caught in Suffolk County

Credit: New York State Department of Environmental Conservation

1. In what month were the most trout found and how many were found that month?

   _____

2. In which three month period were the least total amount of trout caught? _____

   _____

3. Based on the data in the graph, what can you say about summer as opposed to winter as it

   relates to the amount of trout caught? _____

   _____

   _____

Now you will create your own line graph. The data table below shows the average precipitation in the temperate deciduous forest of Staunton, Virginia each month. Use this data table to create your line graph. Don't forget to include:

- A title for your graph

- Titles for your y and x axes

- An appropriate scale and interval for both axes

- Points to show where your data intersects

- A line to connect all your data

Average Precipitation (mm)

Jan	Feb	Mar	Apr	May	Jun	Jul	Aug	Sept	Oct	Nov	Dec
50	50	50	70	90	60	80	90	80	90	70	60

Credit: NASA Earth Observatory

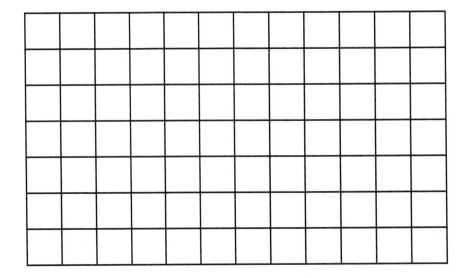

Now write two statements, or observations, about your graph.

1. _____

   _____

2. _____

Name Class Date

Explain

Vocabulary Review

Complete the chart below as you read Pages 48–50 of your textbook. Write the definition of each vocabulary term in your own words. Then, write a note to yourself on how you can remember the meaning of each term. Use the chart to review key concepts after you have finished the Lesson.

Term	Definition	How I Will Remember
Brackish		
Estuaries		
Erosion		
Osmosis		
Osmoregulation		

Use Pages 47–49 in your textbook to help you answer to the Questions below.

1. *Brackish* water can be found in which of the following ecosystems? _____

   a. Coral Reefs

   b. Mangrove Swamps

   c. Polar Regions

   d. Deep Sea

2. Which of the following marine animals would not be found in an estuary? _____

   a. Seabirds

   b. Clams

   c. Polar Bears

   d. Commercial fish

3. Give at least three reasons why estuaries are so important? _____

   _____

   _____

   _____

4. True or False: Salinity levels in estuaries remain fairly constant. _____

5. True or False: Mangrove trees release excess salt through their leaves. _____

Elaborate

In this Lesson you are learning all about the properties of cohesion and surface tension. Below is a cause and effect chart. Use Pages 53–54 to fill out the missing statements. An example has been done for you.

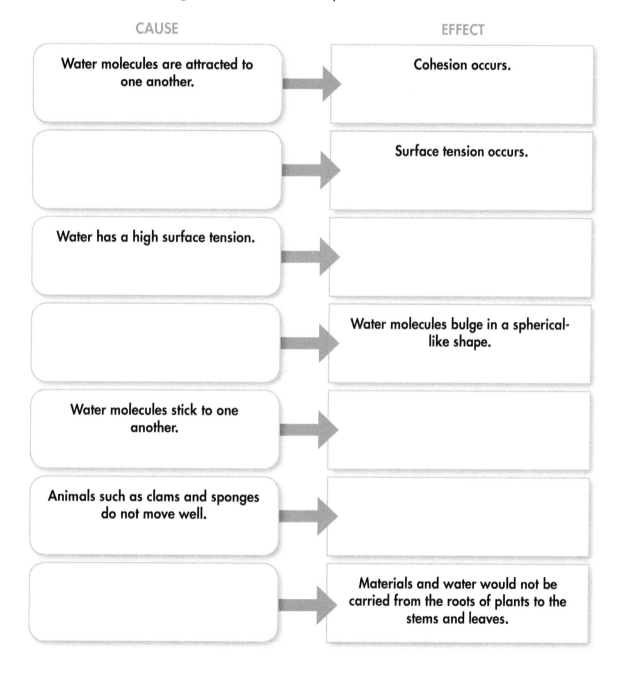

CAUSE

Water molecules are attracted to one another.

Water has a high surface tension.

Water molecules stick to one another.

Animals such as clams and sponges do not move well.

EFFECT

Cohesion occurs.

Surface tension occurs.

Water molecules bulge in a spherical-like shape.

Materials and water would not be carried from the roots of plants to the stems and leaves.

Draw a picture below of how water molecules attract each other via hydrogen bonding.

1. _____ Ionic   a. The ability to carry an electrical charge

2. _____ Metals   b. Need one or two electrons to complete an outer shell

3. _____ Salinity   c. How salt (NaCl) is held together

4. _____ Ionic bond d. The measure of dissolved salts in water

5. _____ Nonmetals e. A compound that consists of atoms that have an electrical charge

6. _____ Conductivity f. Have one or two electrons in their outer shell

7. Define *nonpolar molecules*. Give an example of one type of nonpolar molecule. _____

   _____

   _____

8. Put the following types of water in order from **least** salinity **to greatest**: fresh, ocean,

   distilled _____

9. How does water dissolve salt molecules? _____

   _____

10. On the map on Page 47 of your textbook, where are the majority of the areas of higher

    than average salinity located? the areas of lower than average salinity? Why do you

    think this is the case? _____

    _____

    _____

    _____

Taking notes when you read is an important tool that can help you remember key concepts. One way to take notes and keep new information organized is by using a concept map. Below is one example of a concept map. A **concept map** is a type of graphic organizer used to help us to better understand an idea or topic. In Lesson 3, you are learning about the many unique properties of water. One of these properties is its salinity. Using the boxes below, you will examine "salinity".

As you read about salinity on Pages 45–50 of your textbook, use the concept map below to record key ideas. Then, use this note-taking skill as you complete other sections of the Lesson.

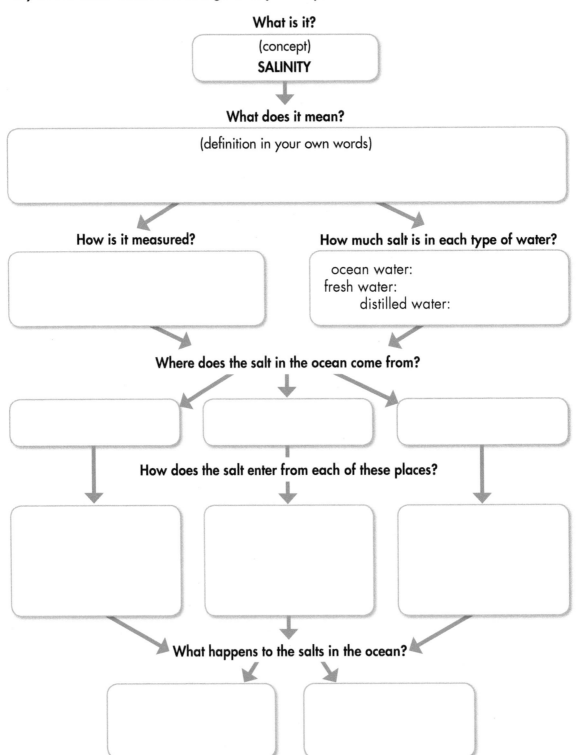

What is it?

(concept)
SALINITY

What does it mean?

(definition in your own words)

How is it measured?

How much salt is in each type of water?

ocean water:
fresh water:
    distilled water:

Where does the salt in the ocean come from?

How does the salt enter from each of these places?

What happens to the salts in the ocean?

Evaluate

Lesson Summary

- Water has many unique properties that shape life on Earth.

- Water on Earth exists in all three states of matter—solid, liquid, and gas.

- Cohesion is the property of water molecules attracting to one another.

- Cohesion on the surface of water is surface tension.

- Water is a universal solvent. Many things, including salts, dissolve in water.

- The salt in the ocean comes from minerals in the atmosphere, rivers and streams, and volcanoes and vents under the seafloor.

- All living things depend on water for survival.

- Marine organisms use and depend on the properties of conductivity, salinity, cohesion, and density, in different ways to meet their needs.

Review key concepts of the Lesson by returning to the anticipation guide that you filled out at the beginning of the Lesson. Review each statement again. Decide if you still agree with your original answer, or if you would like to change your response. In the Explanation column, write a one-sentence reason explaining why the statement is true or changing the statement so that it is correct.

Statement	Agree/Disagree	Explanation
Metals are one of the components of salt.		
Most of the salt in the ocean comes from decaying organisms.		
Many materials can dissolve in water.		
Marine organisms require fresh water to live.		
The salt content of the ocean varies a lot from one place to another.		

Statement	Agree/Disagree	Explanation
Marine mammals drink seawater.		
The attraction of water molecules between each other is weak.		
Many animals rely on the property of cohesion in order to feed and release waste.		
Salt water has the ability to conduct electricity.		

4 The Ocean Over Time

BIGIDEAS

- Humans have relied upon and utilized the ocean for thousands of years for food, resources, trade, transportation, and recreation.

- Scientific inquiry is a cyclical process that scientists employ to learn about our world.

Engage

Activate Prior Knowledge

In this Lesson, you will learn about ways in which humans have relied upon and utilized the ocean for thousands of years. Before reading and trying the activities in your textbook, use the chart below to record what you already know about this topic. After you complete the Lesson, use the chart to record new information you learned.

Read each Question below and think about what you already know about the topic. Write a few ideas, thoughts, or sentences in the What I Know column of the chart.

Question	What I Know	What I Learned
In what ways have people used the ocean over time?		
How much do we know about the ocean and its organisms?		
How do we explore and learn about the ocean?		
What is algae?		

Explore

Build Background

The activity on Pages 59–62 of your textbook asks you to create a timeline. A timeline is a visual guide that helps you quickly see a sequence of historical events. Timelines can help you understand how things happened or changed over time. They can help you make connections between events and see, for example, how one event triggered another. As practice for the *The Ocean in History* activity in your textbook, try first to make a timeline of your life to review this concept.

Timelines have these key elements:

- They are formed from a horizontal or vertical line.

- They show events in chronological order (as points on the line).

- They are drawn to scale.

To get started, fill in the first two columns of the chart below with important events from your life. Begin with the year you were born and end with the current year. Use a new row for each event. You may enter more than one event in the same year if you feel each event is important.

Date or Year	Event	Category

Events on a timeline are often categorized into groups. Some events you recorded in the chart on the previous page might be growth milestones, such as saying your first words. Other events may be related to family life, such as the birth of a sister or brother. Categorizing the events on a timeline helps to organize and show activities that are related.

Look at the events you recorded in the chart and think about how they can be categorized, or grouped. Fill in Category names in the last column of the chart. After recording the titles of your categories, select a different color for each category. Record your color scheme below.

Timeline Key

Now you are ready to construct your timeline. Timelines are formed from a horizontal or vertical line. The line is divided into even intervals, or sections, of time. This is the timeline's scale. The scale should remain the same throughout the timeline. That means the amount of space between years should not change. This helps people see at a glance whether a little or a lot of time has passed between events.

Draw a line on a sheet of paper. Then, determine your scale. Using a ruler as a guide, mark each year on your timeline. See the example below for a model.

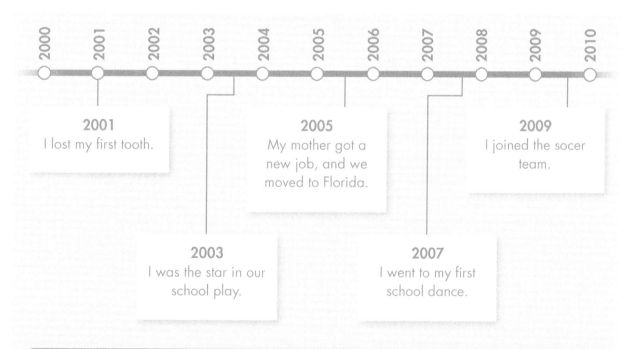

2001
I lost my first tooth.

2003
I was the star in our school play.

2005
My mother got a new job, and we moved to Florida.

2007
I went to my first school dance.

2009
I joined the socer team.

Now you are ready to record events on your timeline. If you included more than one event under a certain year, record the events in the order that they happened. If you did not include an event for a year, leave the year blank, but make sure the year is visible on your timeline. Complete your timeline by lightly coloring each event according to the category color and including a key.

Explain

Review What You Learned

As you learned in the Explore and Explain activities of your textbook, humans have made incredible progress in exploring and learning about Earth's ocean. Nonetheless, much research is yet to be conducted and innumerable questions are yet to be answered about the ocean. Scientists today refer to our ocean as the final frontier.

Read the following selection that summarizes our explorations of the ocean and potential for future research. Then, answer the Questions below to review what you learned.

> "How did the ocean form? Where does it get its power? Why is it blue, brown, or green? What is living in it? ... Certainly these are some of the questions asked thousands of years ago before explorers had access to what we consider, at best, extremely primitive instrumentation and ocean-going vessels.
>
> Today, we have sophisticated technological capabilities that have made the ocean more "visible" and more accessible than it has ever been before. As a result of "new technological eyes", hundreds of new species and new ecosystems have been discovered—some of which may hold the keys to the origin of life on Earth, cures to life-threatening diseases, and knowledge about presently-unknown metabolic pathways for obtaining and using energy to support life here on Earth.
>
> Even though we live on an Ocean Planet, approximately two-thirds of which is covered by water, approximately 95% of the ocean remains unexplored. Recent progress in technology permits us to completely rethink how we conduct exploration and oceanographic studies. Developments in biotechnology, sensors, telemetry, power sources, microcomputers, and materials science now permit the U.S. to ... study the undersea frontier. We need not be limited by weather and blind sampling from ships, but like true explorers, can immerse ourselves in new places and events. The great challenge is getting to the frontier. Once there, we can use many of the same tools and technologies used by scientists studying terrestrial habitats."
>
> Credit: NOAA

1. Here's a fact: We know more about the Moon than our own ocean. Is this surprising to you? Why or why not? How has the information you learned in the Explore and Explain activities in your textbook shaped your response?

_____

_____

_____

2. What are some obstacles that have prevented us from exploring Earth's ocean?

_____

_____

_____

3. How are technologies helping us to overcome some of the obstacles related to ocean research?

_____

_____

_____

4. How have our attitudes about the ocean shifted over time? How are these mental shifts helping us make progress in exploring and learning about the ocean?

_____

_____

_____

5. What new discoveries do you think humans will make about the ocean over the next 50 to 100 years? Predict events you might be able to add to the The Ocean History Timeline in the future.

_____

_____

_____

6. If you were a marine scientist, what aspect of the ocean would you want to study? Why?

_____

_____

_____

Reading Strategy: MAIN IDEA and DETAILS

When you read, it is important to identify the main idea of the selection you are reading. The main idea tells what the selection is "mainly", or mostly about. It is the key concept of the text, or the most important idea being expressed. Often, but not always, the main idea is found at the beginning of a selection or paragraph. Details help to support the main idea often by answering the questions who, what, where, when, why, how, or how many.

As you read the text about algae on Page 64 of your textbook, fill in the Main Idea and Details graphic organizer below. This will help you keep track of and remember what you read.

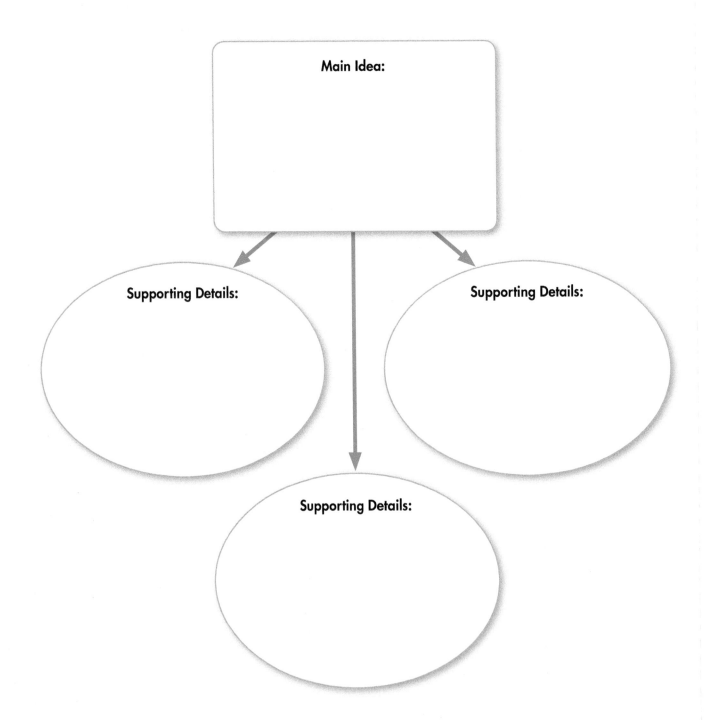

Main Idea:

Supporting Details:

Supporting Details:

Supporting Details:

Name Class Date

Elaborate

Vocabulary Review

Complete the chart below as you read Pages 66–72 of your textbook. Write the definition of each vocabulary term in your own words. Then, write a note to yourself on how you can remember the meaning of each term. Use the chart to review key concepts after you have finished the Lesson.

Term	Definition	How I Will Remember
Scientific inquiry		
Observation		
Data		
Quantitative data		
Qualitative data		
Inference		
Hypothesis		

Term	Definition	How I Will Remember
Experiment		
Conclusion		
Engineering		
Indigenous		

Practice Process Skills: OBSERVE

Scientific inquiry is a process scientists use to answer questions and learn about the world. Scientific inquiry often begins with observations. When we observe, we use our senses to take in information about our world. You might notice the sound of a siren as you walk down the street. This is an observation. You might notice the smell of food cooking in a kitchen. This is an observation, too. Making observations is a foundation of scientific exploration.

Look or walk around your classroom. What are six things you observe? Remember, observations can be made with any of your senses; use at least three senses to come up with the observations.

Anything you notice by touch, taste, smell, sight, or hearing is an observation.

1. _____

2. _____

3. _____

4. _____

5. _____

6. _____

Data from observations are often classified as quantitative or qualitative. Qualitative data offer a descriptive picture of something. The statements are true facts, but do not involve any type of measurement. Quantitative data, on the other hand, are data collected from measurements. Quantitative data always involve numbers or amounts of some kind.

Read the passage below about dolphins. Circle or highlight the data included in the passage as you read. Then, use the chart below to classify the data as qualitative or quantitative.

Scientists in Florida conduct an annual Dolphin Watch. Traveling aboard a research vessel, they tag 100 dolphins, assign each dolphin a number, and make observations about the dolphins' behavior over the course of a year. The dolphins are not hurt in any way, and they usually form a bond with the scientists.

Some dolphins are sighted more than others. Dolphin number 79, for example, was a social creature who stayed close to her home near the NASA Causeway. Number 79 was a friendly female dolphin who was always playful. Scientists were often worried that Number 79 was not timid enough around humans. In the same year that Number 79 was tagged, she was sighted by scientists 25 times, and she was sighted by the general public 93 times. There were 105 photos taken of Number 79 the year she was tagged. Number 79 even got her photo on the front page of a local newspaper.

Qualitative Observations	Quantitative Observations

Evaluate

Lesson Summary

- For thousands of years humans have relied upon the ocean for food, resources, transportation, and recreation. Humans continue to rely upon the ocean today.

- Although only 95% of the ocean has been explored, scientists have been researching the ocean and everything in it for centuries.

- Technologies have helped people explore and learn about the ocean. As technologies improve and become more sophisticated, we become more able to research the ocean and its inhabitants.

- People's attitudes about the ocean have shifted over time as we learned more about its value and need of protection. Laws and agencies have been created to help protect the ocean and its resources.

- Scientific inquiry is a cyclical process scientists use to learn about the world. Scientific inquiry involves making observations, asking questions, forming hypotheses, conducting research and experiments, drawing conclusions, and asking more questions.

Lesson Review

Complete the graphic organizer below to record the main ideas of the Lesson in your own words. Then, turn back to Page 37 of this workbook and record information you gained from this Lesson in the What I Learned column of the chart.

How have the ways that humans use the ocean changed over time?	How do humans learn about the ocean?

5 Migrations of the Sea

BIGIDEAS

- Scientists from around the world use satellite technologies to track marine animals.

- Scientists not only follow the journeys of marine animals, but also monitor the physical parameters that affect their movement, such as food, temperature, landforms, and human activities.

Engage

Activate Prior Knowledge

In this Lesson you will learn about the technologies scientists use to study and gather data about marine animal migratory paths.

Before reading and trying the activities in your textbook, answer the following Questions to review what you already know about the Lesson content.

1. What is migration? _____

   _____

   _____

2. What are some animals that migrate over the course of a year? _____

   _____

   _____

3. Why would some animals need to migrate? _____

   _____

   _____

Explore

Build Background

The activity on Page 82 of your textbook asks you to create a plotting map from data. A plotting map is a geographical map on which you can show a path or travel that happened over time. Plotting maps show data in a visual way and enable us to analyze and understand information about an object or animal's movement more easily.

When you create a plotting map of a journey or movement, you need to have two pieces of information: the object's location and the date or time at which it was at that location. An object's location is often described in terms of latitude and longitude. Latitude and longitude lines are imaginary lines that people developed to help locate places on the surface of Earth. Lines of latitude run north and south around the globe parallel to the Equator. The Equator is represented as 0° latitude. Lines of longitude run east and west around the globe parallel to the Prime Meridian.

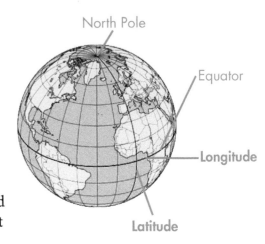

Before trying the activity in your textbook, review latitude, longitude, and the features of a plotting map by studying the map below and answering the Questions that follow on the next page.

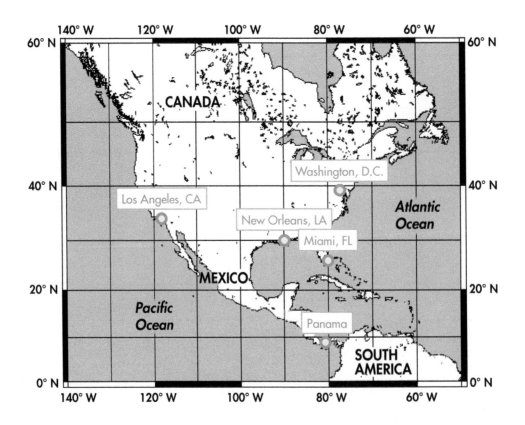

1. What are the approximate coordinates for the following cities?

	Latitude (° N)	Longitude (° W)
1. Washington, D.C.	_____	_____
2. Miami, FL	_____	_____
3. Los Angeles, CA	_____	_____
4. New Orleans, LA	_____	_____
5. Panama	_____	_____

2. Using the same map, plot each of the following locations from a student's journey.

	Latitude (° N)	Longitude (° W)
Day 1	25° N	80° W
Day 2	30° N	90° W
Day 4	35° N	100° W
Day 5	38° N	105° W
Day 7	38° N	122° W

3. Where did the student travel? _____

_____

4. How might the student have traveled? _____

_____

5. Did the student travel the same distance every day? _____

_____

Review What You Learned

After reading Pages 80–81 of your textbook, answer the following Questions to review what you learned.

1. Why is it easier to tag a female Leatherback Sea Turtle than a male? _____

   _____

   _____

2. Describe an adult Leatherback Sea Turtle. _____

   _____

   _____

3. From where have Leatherback Sea Turtles been known to swim (migrate)? _____

   _____

   _____

4. What is the diet of the Leatherback Sea Turtle? _____

   _____

   _____

5. How often do Leatherback Sea Turtles reproduce? _____

   _____

   _____

6. Leatherback Sea Turtles are endangered. Approximately how many nesting females are there worldwide? Why is it difficult for us to determine the size of the male population?

   _____

   _____

   _____

Name Class Date

Explain

Vocabulary Review

Complete the chart below as you read Pages 83–93 of your textbook. Write the definition of each vocabulary term in your own words. Then, write a note to yourself on how you can remember the meaning of each term. Use the chart to review key concepts after you have finished the Lesson.

Term	Definition	How I Will Remember
Uplink		
Downlink		
Natural satellite		
Artificial satellite		
Remote sensing satellite		

Term	Definition	How I Will Remember
Polar satellite		
Geostationary satellite		
Pop-up archival tag		
Satellite relay data logger (SRDL)		
Remote sensing		
Pixel		

Reading Strategy: TAKING NOTES

Remember that taking notes when you read is an important tool that can help you remember key concepts. One way to take notes and keep new information organized is by using a concept map such as the one below.

As you read about satellites on Pages 86–87 of your textbook, use the concept map below to record the key ideas of the text.

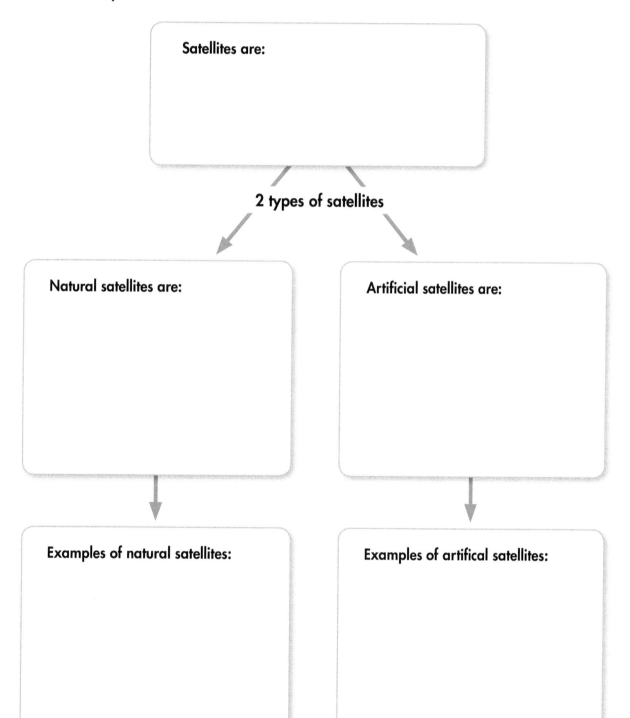

Satellites are:

2 types of satellites

Natural satellites are:

Artificial satellites are:

Examples of natural satellites:

Examples of artifical satellites:

Reading Strategy: COMPARE and CONTRAST

On Pages 88–89 of your textbook, you are reading about three kinds of satellite transmitters that are used to track animals and conditions of the ocean. Comparing and contrasting technologies such as these can help you better understand their uses and limitations. Remember when we compare, we tell how things are alike. When we contrast, we tell how things differ.

Complete the Compare and Contrast Matrix below as you read Pages 88–89 of your textbook.

	Smart Position Tags (SPOT)	Pop-up Archival Tag ('Pop-up Tag')	Satellite Relay Data Logger (SRDL)
How is it used?			
What are some animals it is used to track?			
How is the data collected?			

Review What You Learned

After reading Pages 90–93 of your textbook, answer the following Questions about satellite imagery and scientific discoveries to review what you learned.

1. Define remote sensing in your own words. _____

   _____

2. What can be seen about an animal in a satellite image? What cannot be seen? _____

   _____

3. What type of scientists interpret the information from satellite images? What do they

   each specialize in? _____

   _____

   _____

4. What is a pixel? What two words is it a combination of? _____

   _____

   _____

5. Study the images in Figure 5.31 on Page 91 of your textbook. What do the images

   represent? How do they differ from one another? _____

   _____

   _____

6. How did satellite imagery and the tagging of the Black-footed Albatross lead to a

   surprising discovery? _____

   _____

   _____

Elaborate

Visual Literacy: Reading Maps

Earlier in the Lesson you practiced plotting data on a map. Plotting maps are useful tools in marine science to track animals and show their movement.

Look at the map below. Then, answer the Questions that follow to practice your map reading skills.

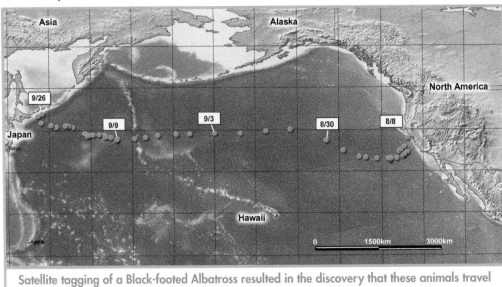

Satellite tagging of a Black-footed Albatross resulted in the discovery that these animals travel throughout the North Pacific.

1. Read the caption. What does the map show? _____

_____

2. Where did the Albatross start its journey? How can you tell? _____

_____

3. Where did the Albatross end its journey? How can you tell? _____

_____

4. On what date did the Albatross' journey end? _____

_____

5. How long did it take the Albatross to make this journey? _____

_____

Evaluate

Lesson Summary

- Many marine animals travel great distances through Earth's ocean, while others move on a much smaller scale.

- Polar and geostationary satellites are human-made satellites that provide scientists with data for tracking and studying marine animals and environmental data.

- Scientists collect data about an animal's location, how deep it dives, and conditions of the water such as temperature and salinity as a means of studying and learning about animal movement and behavior.

- Scientists attach satellite transmitters, or tags, to different marine animal species to help learn about their travels as they migrate across the ocean. Different transmitters are placed on marine animals according to the animal's behaviors.

- Researchers from various backgrounds (e.g., geologists, meteorologists, biologists) study and draw conclusions about the movement of marine animals. Researchers consider conditions such as water temperature and weather patterns as they analyze migratory data.

- Advancements in technology have provided scientists with the opportunity to study marine animals that they otherwise could not observe. This has led to the revision of original hypotheses and ideas.

Organize Your Thoughts

The activity on Page 95 of your textbook asks you to teach others about the Nature of Science. Before you begin creating your final product, organize your thoughts and ideas using the table that follows on the next page. The characteristics of science are listed in the first column. Explain each of these in your own words. Then, provide examples from this Lesson to illustrate your points.

Characteristics of the Nature of Science	What does this mean to you?	Examples from Lesson 5
Science is based on observations, which lead to inferences.		
Science is a cyclical process.		
Science is a creative process.		
Science is subject to change.		
There is a relationship between science and culture.		

Explore the Seafloor

BIGIDEAS

- The ocean floor has varied and distinct surfaces much like those found on land.

- Satellites orbiting Earth, as well as sonar technology, are used to map the seafloor.

- The study of the seafloor and the features found underwater is called bathymetry.

Engage

Activate Prior Knowledge

In this Lesson, you will learn that the ocean floor is not flat but in fact has many features. Many of the seafloor features may seem new, but you are probably already familiar with them as features on land. Some features you see on land may have been under the sea when Earth was still forming millions of years ago.

The shape of Earth's land is called "topography". Topography also refers to the features on planets, moons, and asteroids. When surfaces under the water are described, the term used is "bathymetry".

Illustrate three landforms that you know. Then, list three or more adjectives that describe the landform. If possible name one or more examples of the landform (e.g., Mt. Everest, Grand Canyon).

Drawing of Landform 1	Drawing of Landform 2	Drawing of Landform 3
Descriptions and Examples:	Descriptions and Examples:	Descriptions and Examples:

Explore

Practice Process Skills: MAKE MODELS

The activity on Pages 102–104 of your textbook asks you to create a model of a seafloor. A model is a visual or physical representation of something. Models are important tools for scientists because they help scientists visualize things that are very complex, very small, or very large. They will also help you understand that the seafloor has many features, much like you might find on land.

There are many kinds of models. For the lab in your textbook, you will build a three-dimensional model. Three-dimensional models, or physical models, can show both how something looks and how something works.

Models are often used to show:

- An enlarged version of something tiny, such as a cell.

- A smaller version of something vast, such as the solar system.

- A version of something that cannot be directly observed, such as Earth's inner layers.

In preparation for the activity in the textbook, think about models and how they work. Then, record how you might model each of the features described below. Tell what materials you would use for your model.

1. A gently sloping land area _____

   _____

2. An underwater mountain range _____

   _____

3. A steep-sided canyon _____

   _____

4. An underwater mountain with a flat top _____

   _____

5. A flat, featureless plain _____

   _____

Math Mini-Lesson

After building your seafloor model, you are asked to graph the distance vs. depth of another group's model. This line represents the distance from the coast. The model tells the depth of the ocean at each measured distance. Graphs show data in a visual way and help us to see and interpret relationships in data quickly. A line graph is a type of graph used to compare two pieces of related data, or variables.

Line graphs include these key features:

- A title that tells what the graph is about.

- Two labeled axes that show the variables being compared.

- A scale that shows how each variable is measured.

- Data points that show the relationship between the variables.

Distance (kilometers)	Depth (meters)
0	0
50	-3,500
100	-4,000
150	-5,000
200	-8,000
250	-8,500
300	-10,000
350	-10,000
400	-8,500
450	-8,500
500	-8,000
550	-7,000
600	-4,000
650	-3,000
700	-2,000

Use the sample data (left) to practice making a line graph below. Notice that distance is shown along the x-axis (the horizontal axis). Depth is shown along the y-axis (the vertical axis). To start your graph, find 0 on the x-axis, and 0 on the y-axis. Draw a point or dot on this spot. Next find and put your finger where 50 kilometers is on the x-axis. Trace your finger straight down the graph until you come to 3,500 meters on the y-axis. Draw a point or dot on this spot. Continue plotting the remaining numbers from the table in this way. Then, draw a line to connect the points.

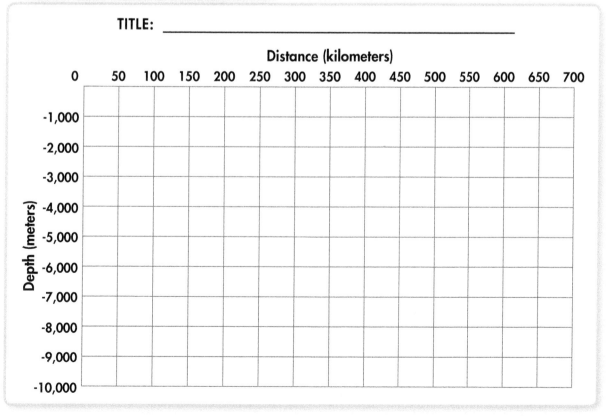

Use the graph you created on the previous page to answer the Questions below.

1. Why does the "zero" depth line start at the top of the scale? _____

_____

2. The first point on the graph has a depth of 0 meters and a distance of 0 kilometers. What

does this mean? _____

_____

3. How is depth measured on the graph? _____

_____

4. How is distance measured on the graph? _____

_____

5. What is the deepest depth shown on the graph? At what distance does this occur?

_____

_____

6. Describe the seafloor feature that you graphed. _____

_____

7. What seafloor feature might this graph represent?

_____

_____   **Hint:** The average depth of the
                                            ocean is 4,000 meters. This feature
_____   would represent one of the deepest
                                            parts of the ocean.

Explain

Reading Strategy: MAIN IDEA and DETAILS

When you read, it is important to understand the main ideas of the selection you are reading. Remember, the main idea tells what the selection is "mainly", or mostly about. Details often help to support the main idea by answering the questions who, what, where, when, why, how, or how many.

On Pages 105–112 of your textbook, you will learn about ways in which scientists map the ocean floor. As you read, complete the 5-4-3-2-1 graphic organizer below to record some main ideas and details of the text.

Five Key Ideas
1.
2.
3.
4.
5.
Four Facts Related to the Main Idea
1.
2.
3.
4.
Three New Words and Their Meanings
1.
2.
3.
Two Facts You Already Knew
1.
2.
One Question You Still Have
1.

Math Mini-Lesson

On Pages 105–108 of your textbook, you learned that scientists measure ocean depths using sound waves or sonar. Sonar instruments on ships transmit a sound pulse quickly into the water. When the pulse hits the ocean floor, the sound echoes back. Sound travels through seawater at a speed of 1,500 meters/second. By measuring the time it takes for the sound to travel through the water and be reflected back to the boat, scientists can do a simple calculation and determine sea depth.

Review the formula below. Then, answer the Questions that follow.

Formula for Calculating Sea Depth:

Sea Depth (SD) = $\frac{1}{2}$ × Time (T) × Velocity (V) or D = $\frac{1}{2}$TV

Here's an example. Suppose it took 10 seconds for a sound pulse to travel through the water and return to the sonar instrument. You could calculate sea depth as follows:

Step 1: Insert the correct numbers into the formula.

D = $\frac{1}{2}$ (10 seconds) (1,500 meters/second)

Step 2: Multiply the numbers in parentheses.

(10 seconds) (1,500 meters/second) = 15,000 meters

Step 3: Divide by 2 to solve.

15,000 meters ÷ 2 = 7,500 meters

Use the formula above to practice calculating sea depths from sonar data. Show all steps in your calculations and be sure to label your answer with the correct units.

1. Calculate sea depth if it takes 20 seconds for sound to be sent and returned by sonar.

2. Calculate sea depth if it takes 25 seconds for sound to be sent and returned by sonar.

3. Calculate sea depth if it takes 30 seconds for sound to be sent and returned by sonar.

Elaborate

Visual Literacy: Reading Diagrams

The diagram on Page 118 of your textbook shows approximate maximum depths to which some air breathing species dive in comparisson to seafloor features. Diagrams such as this are often used in science to show information in a visual way. Being able to read and understand information in diagrams is an important skill.

Complete the table below with information from the diagram. Add animal species, seafloor features, and depths, as needed. Then, answer the Questions that follow.

Animal Species and Seafloor Features	Depths (in meters)
Gray Seal	
	130 meters
	150 meters
Hawaiian Monk Seal	
	1,000 meters
	2,000 meters
Average depth of the ocean	
	11,000 meters

1. Why do you think penguins dive to the same depth of the continental shelf?

   _____

   _____

2. Gray Whales are filter feeders that mainly eat small, shrimp-like animals called amphipods. Why do you think Gray Whales dive only to about 150 meters?

   _____

   _____

3. Why don't the marine species shown in the diagram dive beyond 4,000 meters?

   _____

   _____

Lesson Summary

- The ocean floor has many features including continental shelfs, mid-ocean ridges, abyssal plains, trenches, continental slopes, seamounts, continental rises, and submarine canyons.

- The study of sea depths and their features is called bathymetry.

- Models are important scientific tools; they help scientists study things that are very complex, very large, or very tiny.

- Only 5% of the ocean has been explored, yet throughout history people have been interested in learning about the seafloor. Understanding the seafloor is important for creating shipping routes, maintaining national security, and studying marine animals.

- Early seafarers measured the depth of the seafloor with simple weights attached to lines called plumb lines.

- After World War I, the military began to use sonar technology to measure ocean depths. Sonar equipment set up on ships sent sound waves to the ocean floor. The time it took for the sound to return to the ship was recorded and used to calculate ocean depth.

- Today sophisticated sonar such as side scan sonar and multibeam sonar helps us map the ocean floor and locate things deep in the ocean, such as shipwrecks.

- Orbiting satellites are efficient instruments for mapping the seafloor today because they can scan large areas of the ocean. The best bathymetry maps are created by data collected from a combination of satellite and sonar data.

- Understanding bathymetry helps scientists explain the movements of marine animals.

Lesson Review

Review seafloor features by recording the correct descriptions from those listed below into the blanks in the table. Some descriptions may go in more than one box.

gently sloping land area   bottom of steep slope   underwater mountain range

plunges deep below seafloor   underwater valley   flat, featureless plain

edge of continent down to seafloor   has peak or flat top   deepest feature of ocean

along or near the edges of continents   steep slope   underwater mountain

hill of sediment   steep-sided   makes up large part of seafloor

Seafloor Feature	Descriptions
Continental Slope	
Mid-ocean Ridge	
Seamount	
Abyssal Plain	
Submarine Canyon	

Seafloor Feature	Descriptions
Continental Rise	
Continental Shelf	
Trench	

Give two reasons why understanding sea depth or bathymetry is important when tracking marine animals.

1. _____

   _____

   _____

   _____

2. _____

   _____

   _____

   _____

7 The Formation of the Ocean

BIGIDEAS

- Through the movement of crustal plates, Earth and its ocean have changed over time.

- The Theory of Plate Tectonics explains how geologic features on Earth's surface and seafloor were created and how they have changed.

- This theory illustrates the Nature of Science, in which hypotheses are formed, data are collected, and ideas are re-examined over time as new evidence becomes available.

Engage

In this Lesson you will learn about plate tectonics and how features of the seafloor were formed. Use the chart below to record what you already know about these topics. After you complete the Lesson, use the chart to record new information you learned.

Before reading and trying the activities in your textbook, think about the Questions below. Record what you know about each topic in the What I Know column of the chart.

Question	What I Know	What I Learned
Have the continents always had their current shape and configuration?		
How do the continents move?		
How are features of the seafloor, such as trenches, ridges, and abyssal plains formed?		
What are scientific theories?		

Explore

Build Background

The activity on Pages 122–123 of your textbook asks you to explore ways in which the ocean and land have changed over time. Scientists explain these changes with the Theory of Plate Tectonics. It is likely that you have learned something about Earth changes in previous science classes. Recall that Earth's crust, the outermost layer of Earth, is made up of huge rocky plates. These plates "float" atop Earth's mantle, an inner layer of Earth made up in part of molten (melted) rock. The plates can bump, slide past, or pull away from one another in many ways. When they do, the shape of Earth's land can change.

Read the paragraphs below to review vocabulary terms that describe crustal movement. Then, do the activities that follow to help build your background knowledge of this subject.

"The junction of two tectonic plates is known as a plate boundary. Where two plates slide horizontally past each other, the junction is known as a *transform plate boundary*. Movement of the plates causes huge stresses that break portions of the rock and produce earthquakes. Places where these breaks occur are called faults. A well-known example of a transform plate boundary is the San Andreas Fault in California.

Where tectonic plates are moving apart, they form a *divergent plate boundary*. At these boundaries, magma (molten rock) rises from deep within Earth and erupts to form new crust on the lithosphere. Most divergent plate boundaries are underwater (Iceland is an exception), and form submarine mountain ranges called "oceanic spreading centers" or "mid-ocean ridges."

If two tectonic plates collide more or less head-on, they produce a *convergent plate boundary*. Usually, one of the converging plates moves beneath the other in a process called *subduction*. Subduction produces deep trenches, and earthquakes are common. As the sinking plate moves deeper into the mantle, increasing pressure and heat release fluids from the rock causing the overlying mantle to partially melt. The new magma rises and may erupt violently to form volcanoes that often form arcs of islands along the convergent boundary. These island arcs are always landward of the neighboring trenches. This process can be visualized as a huge conveyor belt on which new crust is formed at the oceanic spreading ridges and older crust is recycled to the lower mantle at the convergent plate boundaries. The Ring of Fire marks the location of a series of convergent plate boundaries that surrounds the Pacific Ocean basin."

Credit: NOAA

Draw a line to match each type of plate boundary with its definition.

Divergent boundaries   Where crust is destroyed as one plate dives under another

Convergent boundaries   Where crust is neither produced nor destroyed as the plates slide horizontally past each other

Transform boundaries   Where new crust is generated as the plates pull away from each other and magma rises from within Earth

Below are several diagrams of plate boundaries. Label each one as a divergent, a convergent, or a transform boundary.

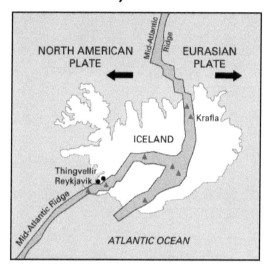

_____

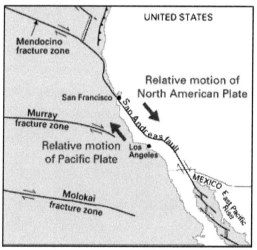

_____

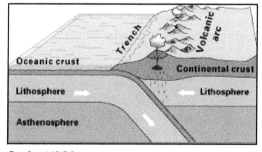

_____

Credit: USGS

Explain

Vocabulary Review

Use Pages 124–129 of your textbook to complete the vocabulary activities below. For Questions 1–7, match each term with the correct definition.

1. _____ Convergent plate boundary

    a. The study of heavenly bodies and their influence on human activities

2. _____ Plate

    b. A high-energy wave caused by earthquakes, landslides, volcanic eruptions, and other natural occurrences

3. _____ Theory

    c. A fracture between plates that slide past each other

4. _____ Convection

    d. A region where two plates collide and one goes under the other forming a trench

5. _____ Transform fault

    e. The culmination of many scientific ideas on a particular topic

6. _____ Astrology

    f. A large piece of the Earth's crust

7. _____ Tsunami

    g. A heat distribution process in which heat is circulated through a liquid or a gas

Draw a line to match each ocean feature to its correct description and location.

Mid-Atlantic Ridge   A deep canyon which runs the length of the Mid-Ocean Ridge

Great Global Rift   An area of the Pacific where large numbers of earthquakes and volcanic eruptions occur

Ring of Fire   A continuous mountain-like structure that runs through the Atlantic Ocean to the southwest coast of Africa

Reading Strategy: SEQUENCE of EVENTS

In the Explain section of your textbook you are reading about the sequence of events that led to Wegener's initial Theory of Continental Drift and its ultimate revisions and acceptance by the scientific community. Remember, a sequence of events describes the order in which something happened. Identifying sequences as you read can help you better understand events and processes that happen over time.

The statements below describe events you read about in your textbook. Write a number on the line next to each statement to arrange the events in the correct order and review what you learned.

_____ Wegener examines research in the fields of geology and paleontology to search for further proof that the continents may have been attached once.

__1__ Wegener studies a map of the world, looking closely at the coastlines on both sides of the Atlantic Ocean. He notices that they could fit together like the pieces of a puzzle.

_____ The Theory of Continental Drift is refined to include evidence that Earth's crust is made up of plates. These plates make up both Earth's continents and the seafloor.

_____ Wegener publishes his book about the Theory of Continental Drift. He cites evidence such as the existence of similar fossil species on varying continents, the matching shapes of coastlines, and the positions of mountain ranges on each continent.

_____ As new evidence is discovered about seafloor features, Wegener's Theory of Continental Drift is strengthened. However, his ideas that land and ocean are different layers of Earth and that land floats on water are shown to be incorrect.

_____ Wegener finds research from paleontologists that provides evidence of a former land bridge between Brazil and Africa.

_____ Wegener's theory sparks debate within the scientific community, and scientists look for new evidence to support or disprove his theory.

_____ At a meeting in Germany, Wegener addresses his fellow scientists and presents his ideas about the Earth's crustal features.

_____ By the late 1960s and early 1970s the evidence supporting Continental Drift was overwhelming, and the theory was accepted by most scientists.

_____ Today the theory is known as the Theory of Plate Tectonics.

Visual Literacy: Reading Diagrams

A variety of diagrams are shown throughout this Lesson to help you understand and visualize key concepts. Remember, diagrams, maps, and graphs are often used in science as tools for communicating information. The diagram of Earth on Page 126 of your textbook is a cross-section diagram. A cross-section diagram shows what you would see if you could slice through an object with a knife. Such diagrams are often used to show what's "buried" beneath an object's surface. Page 126 also shows a cutaway diagram. Cutaway diagrams are another type of diagram that helps you see the inside of something.

Look at the diagrams below and answer the Questions that follow to practice reading information from diagrams.

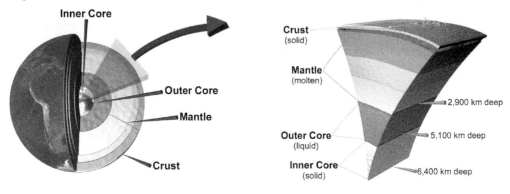

1. What are Earth's four layers? _____

2. What is Earth's thickest layer? _____

3. What is Earth's thinnest layer? _____

4. How do Earth's outer and inner core differ? _____

    _____

    _____

5. How does this diagram help you understand Earth? _____

    _____

    _____

Visual Literacy: Reading Maps

Practicing map reading skills can help you interpret and understand better not only maps, but the concepts and ideas they are trying to communicate. Below is a map that shows Earth's major plates and plate boundaries. This map represents what is currently believed about our planet's crust. Scientific evidence for the locations of plate boundaries includes earthquake, volcano, and seafloor spreading data.

Use the map, what you have learned in this Lesson and your knowledge of geography to answer the Questions below. If necessary, use a globe or world map to help you.

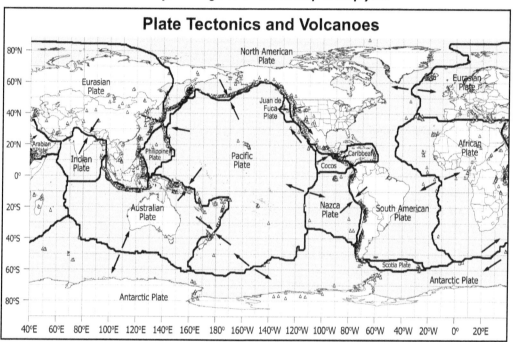

1. How many plates are named on the map? _____

2. Find the United States. On what plate is the country located? _____

3. Which parts of the ocean does the Australian Plate span? _____

4. In what ocean is the Juan de Fuca Plate located? _____

5. Which continents look like they might fit together well? _____

_____

Elaborate

Organize Your Thoughts

In the Elaborate section of your textbook, you and your research team are given the task of reviewing a topic related to the ocean and the Theory of Plate Tectonics. Your team must first read an assigned reading selection and record information that provides oceanic evidence for plate tectonics. You then present your findings to the class.

Use the Questions and table below to organize your thoughts and arrange your information as you work on this assignment.

Research Question	Answer
In your own words, what is the Theory of Plate Tectonics?	
How do scientists decide to research specific topics and investigate specific locations related to plate tectonics?	
What are some places mentioned in the selection you read?	
What geological features are mentioned and how were they formed?	
How do these features relate to plate tectonics and what evidence do they provide for the theory?	
What oceanic processes are described in your selection?	
Why are scientists researching this area?	
What important terms are mentioned in what you read?	
What important events happen in your passage that are related to plate tectonics?	

Evaluate

Lesson Summary

- The Earth's surface consists of many crustal plates, both continental and oceanic, that rest upon the Earth's mantle.

- These plates can be involved in diverging, converging, or transforming boundaries.

- Alfred Wegener's Theory of Continental Drift attempted to explain how similar fossils might have appeared on continents that were located across vast oceans. Wegener believed that the continents had the ability to move together and apart, along the ocean's surface, over time.

- Wegener's theory was renamed the Theory of Plate Tectonics and refined in the 1960s and 1970s.

- The Theory of Plate Tectonics explains how the plates that make up the Earth's surface move when earthquakes, volcanoes, etc. occur and create or destroy land and seafloor features.

- By studying these theories, we can understand how the Earth's ocean and land features were formed and have changed greatly throughout Earth's existence, including how the ocean basins were formed and how the continents have moved.

- Both of these theories illustrate the Nature of Science, in which ideas are tested, data are collected, and information is always being re-examined.

Lesson Review

Answer the Questions below to review the key concepts of the Lesson. Then, return to Page 55 of this workbook and record information you gained from this Lesson in the What I Learned column of the chart.

1. Using the chart you completed for the Explore activity of your textbook, what are several

   ways Earth's surface and ocean features have changed over time? _____

   _____

   _____

   _____

2. Why did the existence of similar fossils on various continents encourage the theory of

   crustal movement? _____

   _____

   _____

3. Compare and contrast the Mid-Atlantic Ridge and the Great Global Rift. _____

   _____

   _____

   _____

   _____

   _____

4. What did most scientists believe about Earth and its features in Wegener's time? _____

   _____

   _____

5. How did arguments and debate among scientists help further Wegener's beliefs? _____

   _____

   _____

6. List at least three pieces of oceanic evidence that support the Theory of Plate Tectonics.

   _____

   _____

   _____

8 Seasons of Change

- Earth's seasonal changes are caused by the tilt of the Earth on its axis and the planet's revolution around the Sun.

- Each season is characterized by the amount of solar radiation received in Earth's hemispheres.

Engage

Activate Prior Knowledge

In this Lesson you will learn about seasonal changes and their causes. Use the chart below to record what you already know about these topics. After you complete the Lesson, use the chart to record new information you learned.

Before reading and trying the activities in your textbook, think about the Questions below. Record what you know about each topic in the What I Know column of the chart.

Question	What I Know	What I Learned
Why are some places regularly warmer or cooler than others in a given month?		
What causes the different seasons?		
How is energy transferred from the Sun to Earth?		
How do marine mammals respond to seasonal changes?		

Explore

Vocabulary Review

Before trying the activities on Pages 143–151 of your textbook, review key vocabulary with the activity below. For Questions 1–9, match each term to the correct definition.

1. _____ Revolution

    a. When the Sun is directly over the Equator, creating 12 hours of daylight and 12 hours of night

2. _____ Hemisphere

    b. A measurement of incoming solar radiation

3. _____ Equinox

    c. An imaginary line around Earth that helps us locate places

4. _____ Solar radiation

    d. The Sun's energy, some of which enters Earth's atmosphere

5. _____ Insolation

    e. The bending of an object

6. _____ Latitude

    f. Gathered together; focused or intense

7. _____ Curvature

    g. One complete trip around the Sun (Earth takes ~365.25 days to move around the Sun)

8. _____ Concentrated

    h. One half of Earth

9. _____ Axis

    i. A real or imaginary line around which an object spins

After completing the demonstration on Pages 143–150 of your textbook use the word bank to complete the following sentences.

Northern Hemisphere	rotation	Autumnal Equinox	diurnal cycle
Southern Hemisphere	Vernal Equinox	Winter Solstice	longest

1. Two times a year the strongest solar radiation lines up directly over the Equator, and everyone on Earth experiences 12 hours of day and 12 hours of night. One of these days is the _____, which occurs on September 22 or September 23. The _____ occurs on March 20 or March 21.

2. The Northern Hemisphere receives its strongest amount of solar radiation and

    _____ hours of sunlight on June 20 or June 21. This is known as

    the _____. The _____ occurs on December

    20 or December 21 when the Southern Hemisphere is receiving the strongest amount

    of solar radiation and the longest hours of sunlight. When the _____

    is experiencing summer, the _____ is experiencing winter.

3. Most parts of Earth experience a period of daylight and darkness over a 24-hour period.

    This is a result of Earth's _____, or the spinning of Earth on its axis.

    This cycle is called a _____.

Organize Information

The Lab on Pages 148–150 of your textbook helps you explore how the curvature of Earth affects the amount of solar radiation received on Earth's surface. Using a chart to organize new information such as this can help you visualize and compare concepts that are related.

After completing the It's All About the Rays *activity in your textbook, use the chart below to record your observations about direct and indirect solar radiation.*

	Sketch a diagram that shows how the curvature of Earth influences solar radiation	Explain your diagram in words
Direct Solar Radiation		
Indirect Solar Radiation		

Name ____________________ Class ________ Date ________

Explain

Vocabulary Review

Complete the chart below as you read Pages 152–157 of your textbook. Write the definition of each vocabulary term in your own words. Then, write a note or draw a picture that will help you remember the meaning of each term.

Term	Definition	How I Will Remember
Insolation		
Angle of insolation		
Differential heating		
Electromagnetic spectrum		
Albedo		
Evaporation		

Review What You Learned

After reading the Explain section of your textbook, answer the Questions below to review what you learned.

1. What does the term *differential heating* mean? _____

    _____

2. Describe in words how Earth experiences differential heating. Then, make a sketch to illustrate your explanation.

    _____

    _____

    _____

    _____

3. In what form does the Sun's radiation travel? _____

    _____

4. How does the Earth's atmosphere protect us from the Sun's radiation? _____

    _____

    _____

5. What is albedo? _____

    _____

    _____

6. What is one way in which heat is transferred back into the atmosphere. _____

    _____

    _____

Elaborate

Reading Strategy: COMPARE and CONTRAST

The Elaborate section of your textbook describes behaviors of Humpback Whales and Harbor Seals. Comparing and contrasting the habits of one animal to another can help you better understand the characteristics of each. Remember, when we compare we tell how things are alike. When we contrast we tell how things differ.

After reading Pages 158–160 of your textbook, use the Venn diagram below to compare the behaviors of Humpback Whales and Harbor Seals. Record traits that seals and Humpback Whales have in common where the circles overlap. Record traits that are unique to each animal in the outer sections of the circles.

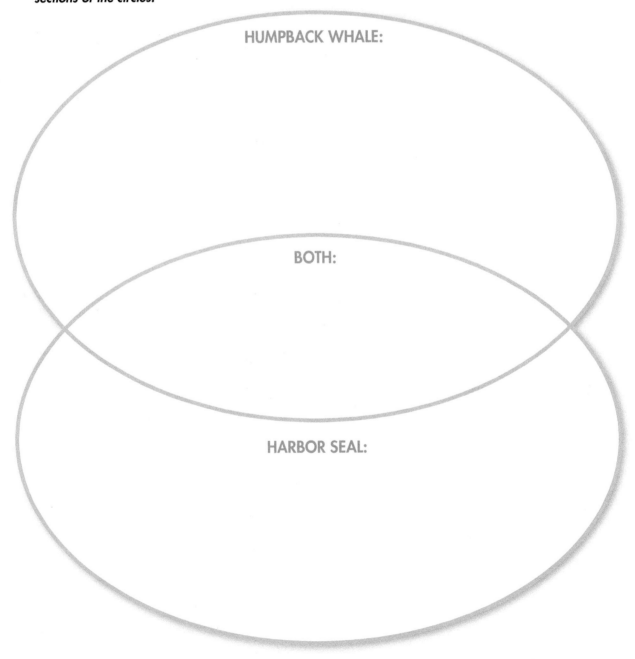

HUMPBACK WHALE:

BOTH:

HARBOR SEAL:

Evaluate

Lesson Summary

- Earth's seasons are a result of result of Earth's tilt on its axis and its revolution around the Sun.

- Seasons are characterized by the amount and intensity of solar radiation received in Earth's hemispheres.

- Due to the curvature of the Earth, different latitudes receive different amounts of radiation on a given day.

- The Sun's energy entering Earth's atmosphere is known as insolation (incoming solar radiation).

- The Suns' radiation travels through space to Earth in the form of electromagnetic waves.

- Earth's atmosphere protects Earth from much of the Sun's radiation.

- Marine mammals respond to changes in the seasons.

Lesson Review

When you have completed the Lesson, try the crossword puzzle on the next page to review key concepts of the Lesson. Then, turn back to Page 65 of this workbook and record information you gained from the Lesson in the What I Learned column of the chart.

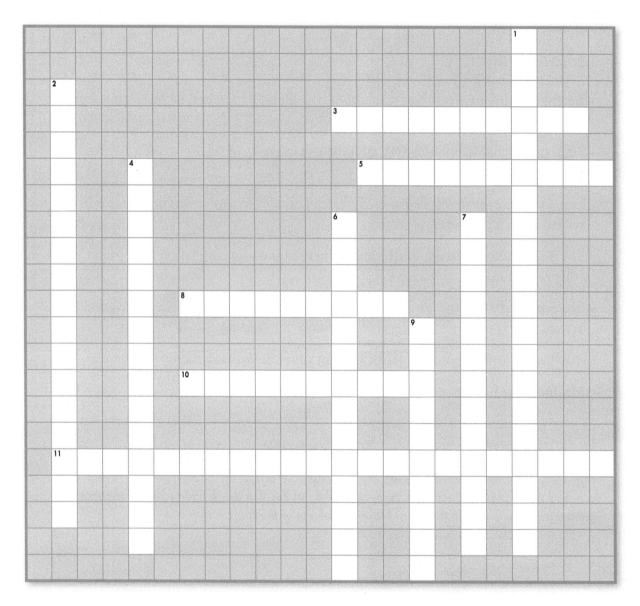

ACROSS

3. One half of Earth

5. It takes Earth 365.25 days to make this

8. Waves used to kill bacteria

10. Waves with the longest wavelengths

11. In the Northern Hemisphere, the Sun's rays are spread out over a greater area

DOWN

1. At the Equator, the Sun's rays are concentrated over a small area

2. The angle at which the Sun's rays reach Earth's surface

4. 12 hours of day and 12 hours of night on September 22 or September 23

6. Sun's energy that enters the atmosphere

7. 12 hours of day and 12 hours of night on March 20 or 21

9. A measurement of incoming solar radiation

9 The Sea Surface: The Great Energy Distributor

BIGIDEAS

- Heat energy in the ocean is distributed through currents.

- The seasons and the exchange of heat in the ocean contribute to environmental changes on the ocean surface.

- Sea surface temperatures and currents affect marine animal movements.

Engage

Activate Prior Knowledge

In this Lesson you will learn about heat and how it is transferred through the ocean. Use the chart below to record what you already know about these topics. After you complete the Lesson, use the chart to record new information you learned.

Before reading and trying the activities in your textbook, think about the Questions below. Record what you know about each topic in the What I Know column of the chart.

Topic	What I Know	What I Learned
What is the main source of Earth's heat?		
What are sea surface temperatures (SSTs)? Why do we study them?		
How do ocean currents form?		
How do currents affect marine animal migration?		

Vocabulary Review

Complete the chart below as you read Pages 164–168 of your textbook. Write the definition of each vocabulary term in your own words. Then, write yourself a note that will help you remember the meaning of each term. Use the chart to review key concepts after you have finished the Lesson.

Term	Definition	How I Will Remember
Sea surface temperature (SST)		
Isolines		
Isotherms		
Isobars		
Radiometer		
Buoy		

Visual Literacy: Reading Maps

Recall from previous Lessons that a map is a picture that shows information about an area. Maps can show the streets and highways in a town. They can show the locations of things, such as exhibits in an aquarium. They can also show features of an area such as mountains, canyons, and lakes. In marine science, maps are used to show conditions of the ocean, movements of currents, and routes of migratory animals, among many other things.

In the Explain section of your textbook, you are reading that satellites measure the infrared heat energy from the top layer of the ocean. This provides us with sea surface temperatures (SSTs). SSTs are the temperatures of the top layer of the ocean. Computers assign a color for each temperature and create a "temperature map".

The map below shows SSTs for the eastern portion of the United States. Color the map according to the key provided.

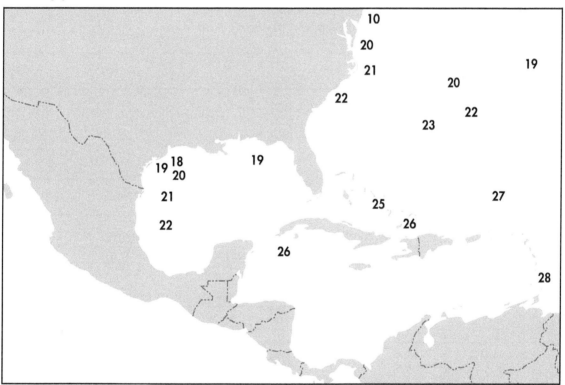

Temperature	0–5 °C	6–10 °C	11–15 °C	16–20 °C	21–25 °C	26–30 °C
Color	purple	blue	green	yellow	orange	red

Use the map from the previous page to answer the following Questions.

1. What do you notice about the SSTs in the Atlantic Ocean along the United States?

    _____

    _____

2. What does the color red represent on this map?

    _____

    _____

3. What does the color blue represent on this map?

    _____

    _____

4. Why is it useful to assign colors to SST measurements?

    _____

    _____

5. What is the purpose of a map key? How does a key help you read a map?

    _____

    _____

6. What would be a good title for this map?

    _____

    _____

Explore

Review What You Learned

After you complete the activity on Page 169 of your textbook, answer the following Questions to review what you learned.

1. Why did you need to put both hot and cold water into the aquarium? Why was the water colored?

   _____

   _____

2. What did you observe during this demonstration? How did the water move?

   _____

   _____

3. Dense materials tend to sink, while less dense materials rise, or float. What can you conclude about the density of cold and warm water from this demonstration?

   _____

   _____

4. Currents are masses of water that move through the ocean. How did the demonstration model the concept of currents?

   _____

   _____

5. Scientists use what they observe to form a hypothesis, a statement that can be tested. After observing the way the warm and cold water behaved in the lab experiment, make a hypothesis about the nature of ocean currents.

   _____

   _____

   _____

Explain

Vocabulary Review

As you read Pages 170–180 of your textbook, define each vocabulary term in your own words. Then, write yourself a note that will help you remember the meaning of each term.

Term	Definition	How I Will Remember
Current		
Surface current		
Convection		
Prevailing winds		
Coriolis Effect		
Gyre		

Reading Strategy: CAUSE AND EFFECT

Page 171 of your textbook describes how currents form. Identifying cause-and-effect relationships in a reading selection such as this can help you make sense of and remember what you read. Recall that a cause is the reason something happens. An effect is what happens as a result.

After reading Page 171 of your textbook, complete the missing causes or effects in the Cause-and-Effect graphic organizer below.

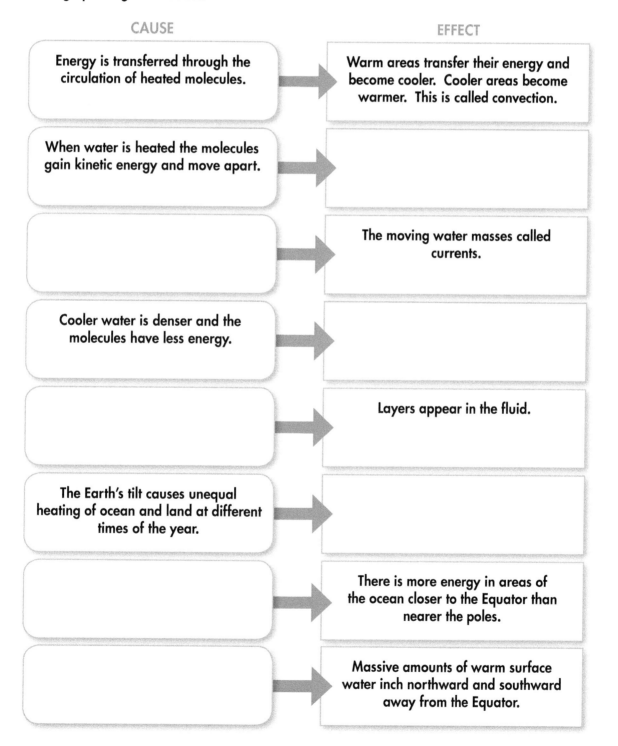

CAUSE	EFFECT
Energy is transferred through the circulation of heated molecules.	Warm areas transfer their energy and become cooler. Cooler areas become warmer. This is called convection.
When water is heated the molecules gain kinetic energy and move apart.	
	The moving water masses called currents.
Cooler water is denser and the molecules have less energy.	
	Layers appear in the fluid.
The Earth's tilt causes unequal heating of ocean and land at different times of the year.	
	There is more energy in areas of the ocean closer to the Equator than nearer the poles.
	Massive amounts of warm surface water inch northward and southward away from the Equator.

Visual Literacy: Reading Maps

Pages 172–179 of your textbook show a variety of maps to aid your understanding of ocean currents. Remember that maps are an important tool in science for showing information.

Look at the map of ocean currents below. Color the solid arrows red. These are the warm currents. Color the dotted arrows blue. These are the cold currents.

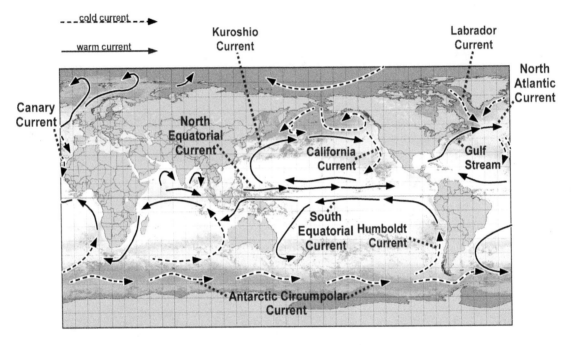

Use the map of ocean currents to answer the Questions below.

1. What do you notice about the location of the warm currents?

   _____

   _____

2. Compare the movement of the warm currents south of the Equator to the warm water currents north the Equator. How do they differ?

   _____

   _____

3. What do you notice about the location and movement of the cold currents?

   _____

   _____

4. The ocean does not flow freely around the globe without interruptions. What happens when water currents hit land masses?

_____

_____

5. What would the ocean be like if we didn't have cold and warm currents?

_____

_____

_____

_____

The map on the right shows Earth's wind patterns. Compare this map of Earth's winds to the ocean currents map from the previous page. Search for similar currents.

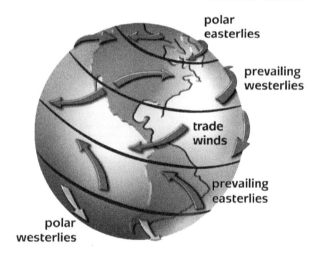

polar easterlies

prevailing westerlies

trade winds

prevailing easterlies

polar westerlies

6. What do you notice about the movement of ocean and wind currents?

_____

_____

_____

_____

Elaborate

Review What You Learned

The ocean absorbs energy from the Sun and distributes heat energy around the planet. This heat distribution is significant for humans and marine animals.

After reading Pages 181–182 of your textbook, answer the Questions and complete the chart below to review what you learned.

1. What would Earth feel like if the oceans did not absorb heat and move around water?

_____

_____

_____

_____

_____

Marine animals are especially affected by changes in the water. Complete the Cause-and-Effect graphic organizer below by recording three causes for marine animal movements.

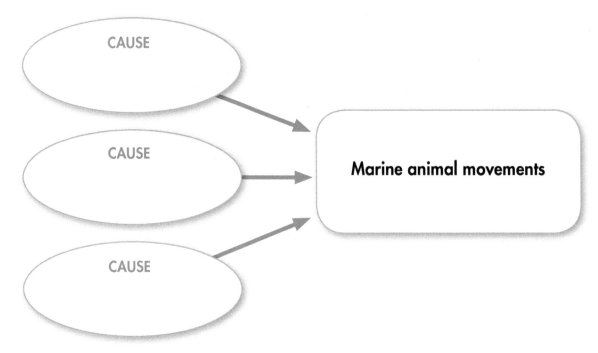

CAUSE

CAUSE

CAUSE

Marine animal movements

Evaluate

Lesson Summary

- Earth's ocean absorbs and distributes much of the Sun's heat energy.

- Density and temperature both affect the flow of warm and cold ocean currents. Warm water is less dense and tends to rise, while cool water is more dense and tends to sink.

- Sea surface temperatures can be collected when infrared energy is measured by satellites.

- Scientific buoys collect data about conditions of the ocean.

- Major surface ocean and wind currents follow similar patterns.

- SSTs and the speed of ocean currents can be measured and used to understand migration and other animal movements.

Lesson Review

Answer the Questions and complete the sentences below to review what you learned in this Lesson. Then, return to Page 73 of this workbook and record information you gained from the Lesson in the What I Learned column of the chart.

1. How is heat energy in the ocean distributed?

   _____

   _____

2. What are six factors that affect the direction and speed of ocean currents?

   1. _____

   2. _____

   3. _____

   4. _____

   5. _____

   6. _____

3. The ocean _____ most heat on Earth.

4. Unequal heating of Earth causes movements of masses of sea water, known

   as _____.

5. Sea Surface Temperatures (SSTs) can be viewed using _____ imagery to tell

   scientists how the heat in the ocean is distributed.

6. Monitoring SSTs and ocean currents helps scientists explain the _____of

   marine animals.

7. The_____causes objects on Earth to curve slightly.

8. Major ocean currents are pushed by_____winds.

9. Use the graphic organizer you completed on Page 79 of this workbook and the information
   from your textbook to write a description of ocean currents and how they form.

   _____

   _____

   _____

   _____

   _____

   _____

10 Energy and the Ocean

BIGIDEAS

- The heat capacity of Earth's ocean plays a role in controlling and moderating Earth's climate.

- Heat and energy transfers affect many systems, including wind and waves.

- Learning about the way heat moves in an open, closed, and isolated system can help us understand the Law of Conservation of Energy.

Engage

Activate Prior Knowledge

In this Lesson you will learn about heat, but there is already a lot that you know about the topic. You experience heat firsthand every day. You have so much experience, in fact, that you can predict what will happen in many situations involving heat and energy transfers. For example, you know that you need heat to cook your food. Heat is also needed for the germination and growth of plants.

Look at the chart below and write a sentence or two to describe your experiences with each example of heat.

Questions About Heat	Answers from Your Experiences
How long might it take a pot of water to boil?	
How might a warm sunny day affect puddles on the ground?	
What happens when you touch a hot pot on the stove?	
Why does a cold drink feel so good on a hot day?	
Why is it harder to run on a hot day than on a cooler day?	
Why can you warm your hands by holding a mug of hot chocolate?	

Explore

Practice Process Skills: MEASURE

The activities on Pages 186–190 of your textbook discuss thermometers and how to use them. We use thermometers to take the temperature of the air, of our bodies, and even of our food. Thermometers often have two separate units of measurement on them, the Fahrenheit and the Celsius scales.

The red liquid inside many thermometers is alcohol. Heat makes the molecules of the alcohol move faster and farther apart. The alcohol expands and rises in the thermometer.

The Fahrenheit scale is used in the United States almost exclusively. On the Fahrenheit scale, the freezing temperature of water is 32 degrees, and the boiling point of water is 212 degrees. The scale is used for the Standard, or English, system of measurement. The Fahrenheit scale is often shown on the right side of the thermometer, and it is labeled with an F.

The Celsius scale is used in science and throughout much of the world. With this metric unit of measurement, the freezing point of water is 0 degrees, and the boiling point of water is 100 degrees. The Celsius scale is labeled on thermometers with a C.

Look at the thermometers below. Write the temperature shown on each thermometer. Write the Fahrenheit and Celsius scales.

1.

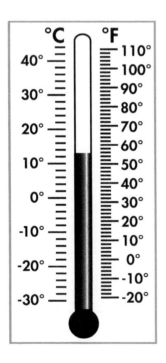

2.

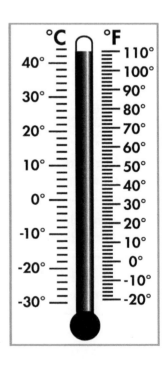

_____ degrees Fahrenheit   _____ degrees Fahrenheit

_____ degrees Celsius   _____ degrees Celsius

3.

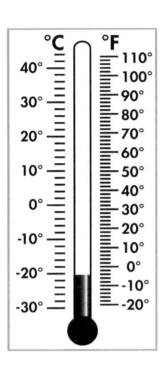

4.

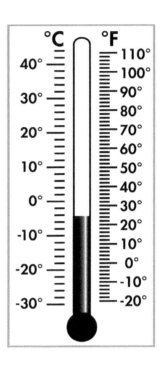

_____ degrees Fahrenheit

_____ degrees Celsius

_____ degrees Fahrenheit

_____ degrees Celsius

5. What is the highest Fahrenheit temperature shown on the thermometer scale above?

   _____

6. What is the lowest Celsius temperature shown on the thermometer scale above?

   _____

7. What is the difference between the Fahrenheit temperatures of thermometers 1 and 3?

   _____

8. What is the difference between the Celsius temperatures of thermometers 2 and 3?

   _____

Math Mini-Lesson

Suppose you have a Fahrenheit reading, but want to know the temperature in degrees Celsius. You can use a formula to convert from one temperature scale to another.

Look at the formula and examples below. Then, answer the Questions that follow.

To convert Celsius to Fahrenheit, use this formula:

$$(°C × 1.8) + 32 = °F$$

When you start with the Celsius measurement,	Multiply by 1.8	Then add 32
40 °C	40 × 1.8 = 72	72 + 32 = 104 °F
21 °C	21 × 1.8 = 37.8	37.8 + 32 = 69.8 °F
-14 °C	-14 × 1.8 = -25.2	-25.2 + 32 = 6.8 °F

To convert Fahrenheit to Celsius, use this formula:

$$(°F - 32) ÷ 1.8 = °C$$

When you start with the Fahrenheit measurement	Subtract 32	Then divide by 1.8
98 °F	98 − 32 = 66	66 ÷ 1.8 = 36.6 °C
47 °F	47 − 32 = 15	15 ÷ 1.8 = 8.3 °C
15 °F	15 − 32 = -17	-17 ÷ 1.8 = -9.4 °C

Use the formulas above to convert the following temperatures.

1. 31 °C = _____ °F

2. 89 °F = _____ °C

3. -11 °C = _____ °F

4. 55 °F = _____ °C

5. 72 °C = _____ °F

6. 112 °F = _____ °C

7. Show the steps you would use to convert 56 °C to a Fahrenheit measurement.

   _____

8. Show the steps you would use to convert -12 °F to a Celsius measurement.

   _____

Explain

Vocabulary Review

As you read Lesson 9, think about each vocabulary word you come across. Try to use each word in a sentence of your own. Then, try the activity below.

Match each vocabulary term with its correct definition.

1. _____ Thermal energy

2. _____ Temperature

3. _____ Heat capacity

4. _____ Habitable

5. _____ Energy

6. _____ Energy transformations

7. _____ Second Law of Thermodynamics

8. _____ Thermal equilibrium

9. _____ Heat energy transfer

10. _____ Conduction

11. _____ Convection

12. _____ Radiation

a. The change of energy from one form to another

b. Energy transfer requiring the direct contact of two materials for heat exchange

c. When the amount of heat going into an object equals the amount of heat going out of the object

d. Radiant, or electromagnetic energy from the Sun, traveling from the Sun to Earth

e. A measure of the average movement of all the atoms, molecules, or ions in a substance

f. The vibration and movement of particles

g. Able to support life forms

h. The amount of energy it takes to increase or decrease the temperature of a substance by one degree

i. The natural and spontaneous flow of heat from an object of higher temperature to an object of lower temperature

j. Energy transfer that occurs by the flow of energy through a liquid or gas

k. The movement of heat from one part of the universe and Earth system to another

l. The ability of an object or a system to do work on another object or system

Reading Strategy: MAIN IDEA and DETAILS

The Explain section of your textbook describes heat and energy. Identifying the main idea and details of the text will help you remember and understand what you read. Remember, a main idea is what a paragraph, lesson, or chapter is "mainly" or mostly about. The details are the facts and ideas that support the main idea.

As you read Pages 190–194 of your textbook, use the concept web below to record the main ideas and details of the Lesson.

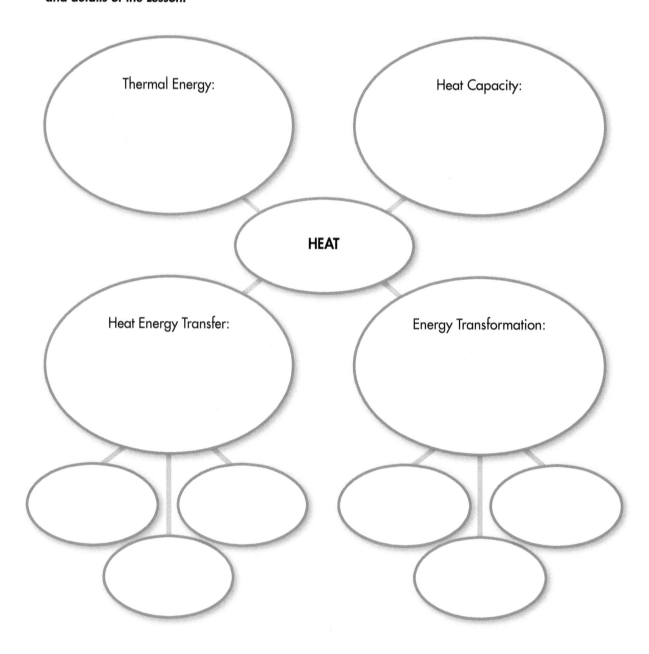

Review What You Learned

After reading Pages 192–194 of your textbook complete the following activities to review what you learned about Energy in the Earth System. Record in the second column of the chart below energy transformations that occur in each example.

Example	Energy Transformation
A candle burns	
A woman rides a bicycle	
A radio plays	
A lamp is turned on	
A motorcycle runs	
A computer runs	

Read the examples of heat transfer below and write conduction, convection, or radiation to describe each one.

1. Heat from the Sun warms the water in a pond. _____

2. A spoon becomes hot after sitting in a hot pot. _____

3. A microwave warms your lunch. _____

4. Hot air rises to the second story of a building on a hot day. _____

5. Ice melts in your hand. _____

6. Cool ocean water becomes warmed near the Poles. _____

Elaborate

Vocabulary Review

Complete the chart below as you read Pages 197–201 of your textbook. Write the definition of each vocabulary term in your own words. Then, write a note to yourself on how you can remember the meaning of each term. Use the chart to review key concepts after you have finished the Lesson.

Term	Definition	How I Will Remember
Law of Conservation of Energy		
Efficiency		
Isolated system		
Re-radiate		
Open system		
Closed system		

Evaluate

Lesson Summary

- Thermal energy is the vibration and movement of particles. Temperature measures the average movement of particles in an object, telling us how "hot" that object is.

- Water requires a large input of energy to increase its temperature. It also requires a large loss of energy to decrease its temperature. Therefore, water is said to have a high heat capacity.

- Energy regularly transforms from one form to another and flows from objects of higher temperature to objects of lower temperature. The transfer of heat will continue until the objects reach the same temperature, or thermal equilibrium.

- Energy is transferred through conduction, convection, and radiation. Conduction occurs between two objects that are touching; convection is the flow of energy through liquids or gases; and radiation occurs when electromagnetic energy radiates from the Sun to warm objects.

- The Law of Conservation of Energy states that energy can neither be created nor destroyed. It can only be transferred or transformed.

- Some energy escapes as heat with each transfer of energy. The more energy that is converted for a specific task, the more efficient the energy transfer is.

- In a closed system, energy is transferred or exchanged with outside systems. In an open system, both matter and energy are transferred or exchanged. In an isolated system, no energy or matter is exchanged or transferred outside the system.

Lesson Review

Answer the Questions below to review the main concepts of the Lesson.

1. How does the Law of Conservation of Energy differ from the Second Law of Thermodynamics?

   _____

   _____

   _____

2. How is energy transferred during conduction?

   _____

   _____

3. How does energy flow between liquids or gases?

_____

_____

4. What is the difference between an open system and a closed system?

_____

_____

5. Describe one example of a transformation of energy.

_____

_____

6. Explain why walking on hot concrete during the summer is painful to the touch.

_____

_____

7. You heat water on the stove and then pour it into two containers. One is a pot of boiling soup, and the other is a room-temperature mug with a tea bag. Which container would experience a greater change in temperature? Why?

_____

_____

8. What are two examples of thermal energy from the Sun being transformed into mechanical energy?

_____

_____

9. What kind of energy system is 100% efficient?

_____

_____

11 Weather, Climate, and the Ocean

BIGIDEAS

- Energy transfer from the ocean to the atmosphere has a major influence on weather and climate.

- Hurricanes are powerful storms that develop over the ocean and are fueled by convection.

Engage

Activate Prior Knowledge

In this Lesson you will learn about powerful hurricanes and how they form. Hurricanes and other severe weather, such as thunderstorms and tornadoes, can be dangerous and destructive.

In the space below, recall a major weather event that you experienced. Describe how it made you feel, what it did to land, and how it affected buildings or wildlife.

_____

_____

_____

_____

_____

_____

_____

_____

_____

_____

Name ______ Class ______ Date ______

Explore

Vocabulary Review

Complete the chart below as you read Pages 205–206 of your textbook. Write the definition of each vocabulary term in your own words. Then, write yourself a note that will help you remember the meaning of each term. Use the chart to review key concepts after you have finished the Lesson.

Term	Definition	How I Will Remember
Air mass		
Climate		
Front		
Wind		
Cold front		
Warm front		

Term	Definition	How I Will Remember
Leeward		
Biogeochemical cycle		

Match each air mass with its correct description.

1. _____ Maritime Tropical   a. A body of cold, dry air that originates over high latitude continents

2. _____ Continental Tropical   b. A body of warm, moist air that originates over tropical oceans

3. _____ Maritime Polar   c. A body of cool, moist air that originates over mid- to high latitude ocean

4. _____ Continental Polar   d. A body of hot, dry air that originates over tropical continents

Use the definitions above to label where these kinds of air masses form on the map below.

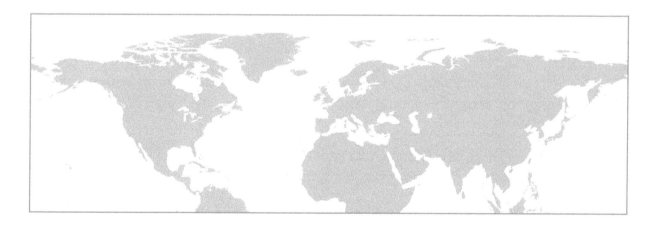

Explain

Reading Strategy: SEQUENCE of EVENTS

Your textbook describes how tropical cyclones (called hurricanes in the United States) develop. Although these storms are called different names in different parts of the world, they have the same structure and process for development. Keeping track of the sequence in which events happen can help you understand processes. Remember, a sequence describes the order in which something happens.

Below are several statements related to hurricane development. After reading about hurricane development in your textbook, number the statements to show their general sequence and review what you learned. The first one has been done as an example.

_____ Light air from the low pressure area rises and heavier, warm air flows toward the area of low pressure.

_____ More air rushes in toward the area of low pressure and the cycle of evaporation and condensation continues, building more energy and larger clouds with circulating winds.

__1__ A low pressure area develops over the surface of tropical water and begins to circulate in a counter-clockwise direction.

_____ The moist air rises. As it rises, it cools, and the water vapor it carries condenses and forms clouds.

_____ The warm air increases evaporation at the ocean's surface. The process of evaporation cools the surface of the water.

_____ The heat of condensation warms the atmosphere and adds energy to the system. The warm air rises higher.

_____ The storm forms an intense eye with thunderstorms wrapping around the center and the strongest wind recorded since it developed.

_____ The storm moves over the ocean, makes landfall and begins to weaken.

Elaborate

Practice Process Skills: ANALYZE DATA

You know that scientists collect and record data. Meteorologists, scientists who study Earth's atmosphere, often collect data about weather conditions such as temperature and precipitation. They analyze the data to understand weather and climate and their causes better. Analyzing data is an important step of the inquiry process. When you analyze data, you look for patterns and relationships between variables. Analyzing data helps you make inferences to explain observations and helps you draw conclusions about hypotheses and research or experimental results. The activity on Pages 221–223 of your textbook asks you to analyze data about weather and climate from different cities in the United States.

Scientists often create graphs from data collected in tables as part of data analysis. Graphs, such as line graphs and bar graphs, are visual tools that help us recognize patterns and relationships quickly.

Before answering the Questions on Page 223 of your textbook, practice analyzing data from one of the cities shown in your textbook.

Jacksonville, Florida

	Jan	Feb	Mar	Apr	May	Jun	Jul	Aug	Sep	Oct	Nov	Dec	Annual
Avg. Max. Temp. (°F)	64.0	67.1	73.3	80.0	86.6	90.6	91.4	91.0	88.1	80.9	72.3	65.6	79.2
Avg. Min. Temp. (°F)	39.9	42.0	47.5	53.2	61.9	69.1	71.1	71.1	68.5	57.1	46.8	41.3	55.9
Avg. Total Precipitation (in.)	4.31	4.86	5.73	3.74	4.30	7.09	8.28	7.28	5.53	3.21	3.35	4.12	61.80

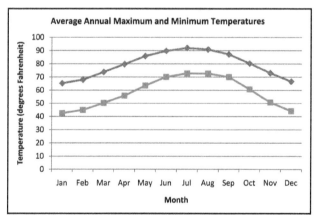

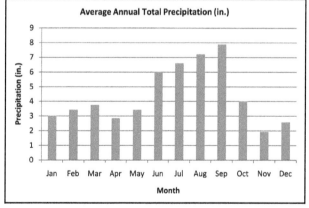

1. What data was collected? _____

_____

2. When are temperatures at their highest in Jacksonville? _____

_____

3. When are temperatures at their lowest in Jacksonville? _____

_____

4. What is the range in average monthly rainfall? _____

_____

5. Is there a relationship between temperature and rainfall? How does rainfall change as

temperature increases or decreases? _____

_____

_____

_____

_____

6. Using the information you learned in this Lesson, can you explain the relationship

between precipitation and temperature? What inferences can you make? _____

_____

_____

_____

_____

_____

_____

_____

Evaluate

Lesson Summary

- Tropical cyclones are severe storms that form over warm, tropical waters. Tropical cyclones develop and move in predictable patterns and tend to form in different regions at specific times of the year.

- Air masses are large bodies of air over Earth's surface that have similar temperature and moisture characteristics.

- Major weather events are common along frontal boundaries when air masses of different types collide or interact.

- There are a global wind patterns in Earth's atmosphere. This is due to heating and cooling of air on our rotating Earth. There is more solar energy reaching the Equator than at Earth's poles.

- The global wind pattern helps steer storms and weather systems.

- Air is deflected to the right in the Northern Hemisphere and to the left in the Southern Hemisphere due to the Coriolis Effect associated with Earth's rotation.

- Climate is the long-term weather pattern of an area.

Lesson Review

Complete the Questions below to review key concepts from the Lesson.

1. Describe how air density is related to the following.

   Hurricanes: _____

   _____

   _____

   _____

   Global wind pattern: _____

   _____

   _____

   _____

Name ____________ Class ______ Date ______

2. Describe how the ocean is related to the following.

Hurricanes: ____________________

____

____

____

____

____

Air masses: ____________________

____

____

____

____

____

Climate: ____________________

____

____

____

____

____

12 Voyage to the Deep

BIG IDEAS

- Pressure, salinity, temperature, density, and the availability of light are environmental conditions that change as you go deeper into the ocean.

- Marine animals that live in, or dive to, great ocean depths have adaptations that allow them to deal with the conditions of the deep ocean.

- Submersibles, CTD (conductivity, temperature, and density) devices, and other advancements in technology allow us to explore the depths of the ocean.

Engage

Activate Prior Knowledge

In this Lesson you will learn about environmental conditions of the deep ocean, how we study these conditions, and how marine animals are adapted to them. Below is a concept web. In the center of the web is the concept you will be studying. Each of the surrounding circles represents one of the environmental conditions that you will read about.

Use the Objectives, the Engage section of your textbook, and information you already know about the ocean to fill in five ocean "parameters" in the circles attached to "The Deep Ocean" below. At the end of the Lesson, you will record facts about each of these conditions in the smaller outer circles.

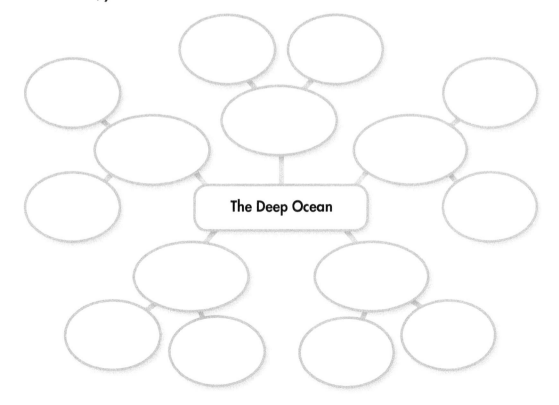

The Deep Ocean

Explore

Practice Process Skills: ANALYZE DATA

The activity on Page 229 of your textbook asks you to create and interpret a line graph from data you collect. Remember, graphs show data in a visual way and are useful tools for analyzing data. They help us to see and interpret relationships and patterns in data quickly. A line graph is a type of graph used to compare two elements of related data, or variables.

Study the line graph below. Then, review the features of a line graph and answer the Questions that follow to practice analyzing data from graphs.

Line graphs include these key features:

- A title that tells what the graph is about.

- Two labeled axes that show the variables being compared.

- A scale that shows how each variable is measured.

- Data points that show the relationship between the variables.

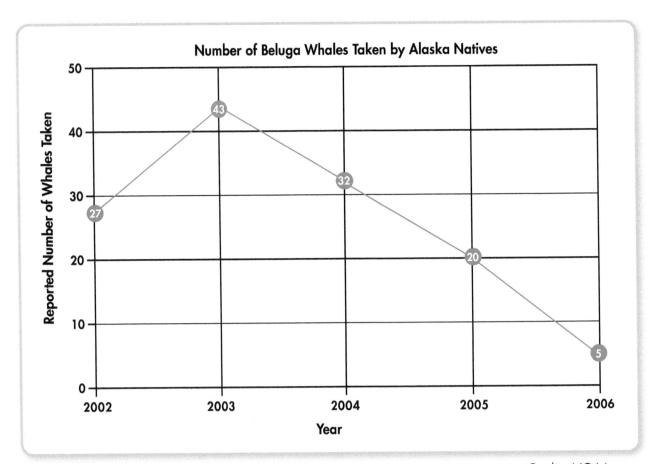

Number of Beluga Whales Taken by Alaska Natives

Credit: NOAA

A title gives us an overview of the information being presented on a graph.

1. What is this graph about? _____

    _____

Each variable in a line graph is shown along an axis. The vertical axis is called the y-axis, and the horizontal axis is called the x-axis. Each of the axes is labeled to show the variables being plotted on the graph.

2. What variable is shown on the horizontal, or x-axis? _____

3. What variable is shown on the vertical, or y-axis? _____

A scale across the horizontal and the vertical axes tells how each variable is measured. For example, if time is a variable you want to plot, then your scale would show seconds, minutes, or another unit of time according to how your data was collected.

4. What scale is used for the x-axis in the graph on the previous page? _____

5. What scale is used for the y-axis? _____

A scale must always include the lowest and highest value of your data and be separated into equal intervals, or parts. Intervals may be counted by 1s, 5s, 10s, etc. depending on what is most useful about the data you are using.

6. What interval is used for the variable shown on the x-axis? _____

7. What interval is used for the variable shown on the y-axis? _____

The points on the graph show the relationship between the variables, or where data from the x- and y- axes intersect. The points are connected with a line to complete the graph.

8. What was the largest number of whales taken? In which year was this number of whales

    taken? _____

9. In what year were the fewest whales taken? _____

10. How is the number of whales taken each year changing? _____

    _____

Now that you know the features of a line graph and know how to analyze the data shown on a line graph, use the data in the table below to practice making a line graph. *Don't forget to include:*

- A title for your graph
- Labels for your y- and x-axes
- An appropriate scale and interval for both axes
- Points to show where your data intersects
- A line to connect all your data

After you have finished creating your line graph, write three observations that you can make about this graph. Write your statements.

1. _____

   _____

2. _____

   _____

3. _____

   _____

Monthly Total Zooplankton

Month	Number of Trout Caught
August	275
September	138
October	294
November	151
December	225
January	150
February	200
March	220
April	298
May	630
June	478
July	870

Credit: FAO

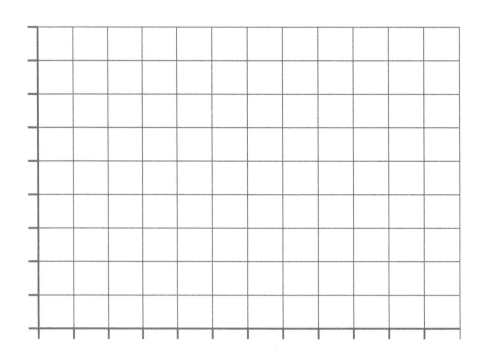

Explain

Read the descriptions below of several different types of Questions to help you become more familiar with the information in this section of the text.

A **"Right There"**, or literal, Question is a type of question where you can go back to the text and the correct answer is "right there". You can take your answer directly from the passage.

Answer this "Right There" Question from the Explain section of your text.

How long does a typical CTD device drop take? _____

_____

A **"Think and Search"** Question is a question which requires you to read the text and then think about how ideas in the passage relate to one another. The information will be found in the text but the answer will have to be written in your own words.

Answer this "Think and Search" Question from the Explain section of your text.

Compare and contrast the difference between how deep Sperm Whales and Leatherback Sea

Turtles dive. _____

_____

_____

_____

Inferential Questions ask you to use your prior knowledge combined with what you have read in the text to make guesses, or predictions, or state an opinion on a particular topic.

Answer this Inferential Question related to the Explain section of your text.

Describe one way that you think global warming might affect the *Global Conveyor Belt*?

_____

_____

_____

_____

The diagram below is similar to the graphs seen in your text on Page 231. Use it and your knowledge of the subject to help you answer the Questions below. On this graph, temperature is represented by the white line.

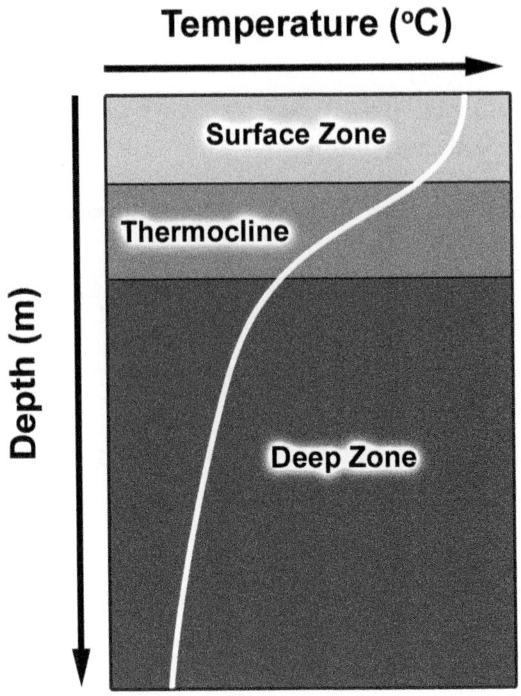

Temperature (°C)

1. According to what you learned in this Lesson, why would the temperature in the Surface

   Zone be the warmest? _____

   _____

2. You have learned that the *Thermocline* is the boundary layer that separates the warmer,

   surface water from the colder water below. What begins to happen to the water's

   temperature as you reach the *Thermocline* layer? _____

   _____

   _____

3. What happens to the water temperature as you travel through the Deep Zone, as shown

   by the white line on the graph? Why does this happen? _____

   _____

   _____

Below is the one of the diagrams from Page 231 in your text. Use it and your knowledge of the topic to help you answer the Questions that follow.

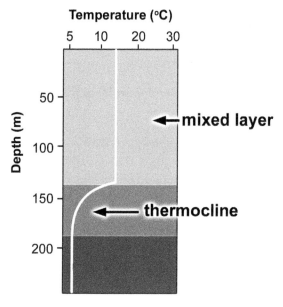

4. What is the temperature in the *mixed layer*, or *surface zone*? _____

_____

5. At what depth does the *thermocline* occur? _____

_____

6. In the thermocline layer, about how many degrees does the temperature change from the

    top of the layer to the bottom? _____

_____

7. In what season were these measurements taken? _____

_____

8. Why might it be important to know when the measurements were taken? _____

_____

_____

_____

Reading Strategy: SUMMARIZING

Being able to summarize during and after reading text is an important tool. **Summarizing** means taking only the key ideas, or main points, out of a larger selection of text and restating them in your own words. Below is a passage about the adaptations some species of crabs make to survive in the deep sea.

Read the selection. Then, we will look for several main ideas from the passage and turn them into a short summary of the passage.

The deepest crab in the Gulf of Alaska is the large-clawed spider crab. Its body is about 10 cm across, but the legs reach up to 50 cm in length. The claw segment of adult males is over a foot long. They look like a giant daddy-long legs spider on steroids. These crabs live down to at least 3,400 m (over 11,000 ft), and yet they have eyes.

Most of the other crab species are restricted to specific depth zones by temperature requirements. The only way they can spread to other seamounts is by releasing swimming larvae that are carried across the sea by water currents. The large-clawed spider crab, though, may be able to descend all the way to the bottom of the ocean. In effect, it probably walks across the seafloor, from Hawaii to Alaska. Because there isn't much food down there, it may feed on foodfalls (i.e., dead animals that fall from surface waters, such as whales, sea lions, or large fish). Crabs can go for long periods without eating. When they find a food source, they can live off it for some time, until it is consumed, then go on their way searching for others. At foodfalls such as this, predator organisms and bacteria may give off phosphorescence (light produced by living organisms) that is detectable by the spider crab's eyes.

Their long legs may be an adaptation for traveling long distances. We have much to learn about deep-water crabs, or other species in the deep sea. They are fascinating and puzzling. They can tell us much about how animals cope with life in the deep sea, but they present new and challenging questions as well.

Credit: NOAA, Adaptations of Crabs to Life in the Deep Sea

In the boxes below, let's list some of the main ideas from the passage. Two boxes have been filled in for you as examples. See if you can find two other important ideas from what you read and fill in the other boxes.

Main Idea	Main Idea	Main Idea	Main Idea

Some of the other ideas you might have written are:

- live at depths of up to 3,400 m (11,000 feet).

- can live off of foodfalls of larger dead marine animals like whales, sea lions, and fish for a long period of time.

- have eyes that can detect phosphorescence given off by predators and bacteria

Now use the lines below to come up with a two-sentence summary using some of the ideas above.

_____

_____

_____

_____

_____

_____

_____

Below is a selection from Page 236 in your textbook. Read it carefully. Then, use the boxes on the following page to write four main ideas from the passage. Turn those four main ideas into a two-sentence summary of this text.

Another characteristic of the deep sea is the lack of visible light. Sunlight does not easily penetrate the ocean's waters. Near the surface, light is absorbed when water molecules vibrate and light energy is converted into heat energy. Some visible light and the various colors of the electromagnetic spectrum are absorbed closer to the surface than others. In fact, the reason that the ocean appears blue is that the red visible light is absorbed quickly by water, whereas the blue light is absorbed more slowly, allowing the color to be scattered back to our eye. The layer of ocean surface water in which light is able to penetrate is referred to as the **photic zone**. The thickness of the photic layer depends on Earth's curvature and the directness or intensity of the Sun's rays, the season, and the turbidity (the cloudiness or haziness) of the seawater.

As shown in the graphic above, the red wavelengths of light are absorbed within the ocean's very top few meters. Red objects, including fish, corals, and even blood, appear grey below the depth where red light has been absorbed. There is no red light energy to reflect back to your eye. To take vivid pictures of brightly colored organisms, like those found in coral reefs, scientists and recreational scuba divers get close to their subjects and use an underwater camera with a bright flash. The flash is white light, which contains all of the visible light wavelengths—including red.

Name _____ Class _____ Date _____

Main Idea	Main Idea	Main Idea	Main Idea

Summary

Lesson 12 Marine Science: The Dynamic Ocean Study Workbook • © U.S. Satellite Laboratory, Inc. All Rights Reserved.

Elaborate

Visual Literacy: Reading Graphs

Earlier in the Lesson, you reviewed graphing skills. Remember that line graphs are used to show two variables in relation to one another. On Page 243 of your textbook are several line graphs. These are slightly different from the line graphs you worked with earlier in this Lesson; they're kind of like four line graphs in one. The x-axis is used to show four different variables—temperature, density, salinity, and fluorescence. Each of these variables is color-coded and has its own scale. All four of the variables are plotted against depth, the variable shown on the y-axis. To read the graph, match the color of one of the lines to its labeled scale on top of or below the graph. Here is an example:

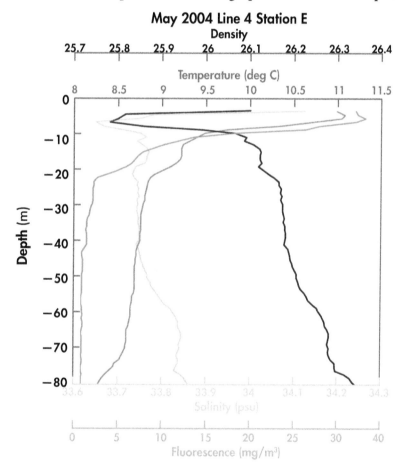

Credit: PRBO Conservation Science and NOAA Cordell Bank NMS

Look at the graph above. Notice that the word density and the scale for density appear in black type above the graph. This helps you know that the black line on the graph represents density at different depths. What variable is represented by the:

Gray line? _____

Light blue line? _____

Dark blue line? _____

The vertical, or *y*-axis, on this graph represents water depth measured in meters. Because we are measuring against sea level and going deeper (down), the numbers we see are negative numbers. The value -60 indicates a depth of 60 meters below the surface of the water.

What does -30 indicate? _____

Which is closer to the surface of the water, -80 or -10 meters? _____

Now read the graph to answer the Questions below.

1. What unit is temperature measured in?

    _____

    _____

2. Put your finger on the dark blue line. When fluorescence = 5 mg/m³, what is the water depth? (Remember to include the negative sign before your answer.)

    _____

    _____

3. At a depth of -2 meters, the salinity (the light blue line) is about 34.1 psu. Then at -5 meters, the salinity is less than 33.7 psu. What happens to the salinity after -5 meters?

    _____

    _____

Evaluate

Lesson Summary

- As you go deeper in the ocean, pressure, salinity, temperature, density, and the availability of light change.

- Temperature decreases with increasing depth. This is because the Sun's rays do not penetrate deeper water.

- Pressure, measured in psi, or pounds per square inch, increases with water depth.

- Water density, which measures how closely molecules are packed together, also increases with depth.

- Water salinity, which is the amount of salt dissolved in the water, first decreases with depth, then increases.

- Fluorescence is a measure of the availability of light. Fluorescence decreases significantly with increasing depth, until it finally disappears.

- Marine animals that live in or dive to great depths for food sources have adaptations, such as bioluminescence and echolocation, which allow them survive in their environment.

- Submersibles, and other advancements in technology, such as CTD (conductivity, temperature, and density) devices allow us to take measurements at different water depths and help scientists to better understand the deep ocean ecosystem.

- The Global Conveyor Belt is a system of deep water currents that connects all the world's ocean basins, provides heat to Earth's Polar Regions and distributes nutrients throughout the ocean.

- The photic zone is the layer of ocean water which light is able to penetrate. The ocean appears blue because blue light is absorbed most slowly and has the deepest penetration depth.

Lesson Review

Return to the concept web you started at the beginning of this Lesson. Record definitions, facts, or other details related to each oceanic parameter in the outermost circles of the web. Then, use your web, text, and the previous workbook pages to help you answer the Questions below.

1. Give two examples of how technology has helped us to discover more about the deep

   ocean. _____

   _____

   _____

   _____

2. What is a thermocline? _____

   _____

   _____

   _____

3. Identify at least three adaptations of Sperm Whales that allow them to survive and feed in

   deep water. _____

   _____

   _____

   _____

13 Photosynthesis in the Ocean

BIGIDEAS

- Microscopic organisms in the water use energy from the Sun to carry out the food-making process of photosynthesis.

- Carbon is cycled through the environment by both living and non-living things.

- Satellite imagery helps us locate and track phytoplankton populations.

Engage

Activate Prior Knowledge

Below is an anticipation guide. It includes statements related to what you will read in this Lesson. Some of the statements are accurate, while others are not. Completing an anticipation guide before you read can help you recall information you know about a topic and become better prepared for reading. When you have finished the Lesson, you will review your responses and compare them with what you have learned.

Before reading the Lesson, review each statement in the chart and record whether you agree or disagree with the statement. Use what you have learned in the previous Lessons to help you make your decisions.

Statement	Agree/ Disagree	Explanation
The purpose of photosynthesis is to produce oxygen.		
Salt water can be used for photosynthesis.		
More than half of the world's oxygen is produced by phytoplankton.		

Statement	Agree/ Disagree	Explanation
Plants get their food from nutrients in the soil, such as nitrogen and phosphorus.		
Most of the carbon dioxide on Earth is found in the atmosphere.		
The ozone layer was created millions of years ago from oxygen released by a type of phytoplankton.		
Satellite images measuring chlorophyll concentration can help us to understand the migration of many marine animals.		
The open ocean is the most productive marine ecosystem.		
Undersea vents and volcanoes provide sources of carbon dioxide in the ocean.		
The oxygen released by photosynthesis helps create the ozone layer which protects us from the Sun's harmful UV rays.		

Explore

Practice Process Skills: DEFINE VARIABLES

When conducting an investigation, we often observe or make measurements of things that change. These are variables. Defining and keeping track of variables in an experiment is important because it helps you analyze and understand your results. As you learned in Lesson 2, there are two main types of variables—independent variables and dependent variables. A third type of variable is a controlled variable.

Below is a list of variables in the **Observing Photosynthesis** *activity of your textbook. Think about each variable and classify it as an independent variable, a dependent variable, or a controlled variable.*

An *independent variable* has these features:

• Is often something that a scientist changes in order to do an experiment.

• Is not affected by other variables.

A *dependent variable* has these features:

• Depends on other factors in the experiment.

• Is often the factor we are trying to learn more about.

• **Amount of light**

• **Type of plant**

• **Addition of carbon dioxide**

• **Amount of water**

• **Size of container**

• **Addition of Bromothymol blue solution**

• **Consumption of carbon dioxide (evidence of photosynthesis)**

---

1. What was the independent variable in your experiment?

   _____

   Hint: Ask yourself, what variable did we change for each flask?

2. What was the dependent variable? _____

3. What were the controlled variables, or the things you tried to keep the same in each part

   of the experiment? _____

   _____

Answer the Questions below to practice defining variables.

Students in Mrs. Smith's 8th period science class wanted to conduct an experiment to see how varying hours of studying would affect test grades on their science midterm.

1. What is the independent variable in this experiment? _____

2. What is the dependent variable? _____

3. What might be some of the controlled variables? _____

   _____

Scientists wanted to test whether mice will make it through a maze with a piece of cheese at the end faster than if there were no cheese.

4. What is the independent variable in this experiment? _____

5. What is the dependent variable? _____

6. What might be some of the controlled variables? _____

   _____

Suppose you wanted to do an experiment to answer this question: How do sea surface temperatures affect the size of phytoplankton populations?

7. What would be your independent variable? _____

8. What would be your dependent variable? _____

9. What variables would you control? _____

   _____

   _____

Name Class Date

Explain

Vocabulary Review

Complete the chart below as you read Pages 251–253 of your textbook. Write the definition for each vocabulary term in your own words. Then, write yourself a note that will help you remember the meaning of each term. Use the chart to review key concepts after you have finished the Lesson.

Term	Definition	How I Will Remember
Autotroph		
Photosynthesis		
Phytoplankton		
Cyanobacteria		

Term	Definition	How I Will Remember
Ozone		
Chloroplast		
Decompose		
Pigment		
Carbon cycle		

Review What You Learned

Below is a chemical equation that illustrates the reactants and products of photosynthesis. Use this graphic organizer to help you record and review important information you learned on Pages 250–251 of your textbook.

Label the missing reactants, materials, and products involved in photosynthesis. Use the word bank to help you fill in the correct terms. Then, write a description or fact about each reactant and product in the boxes below the equation.

PHOTOSYNTHESIS WORD BANK			
Light	Glucose	Enzymes	Nutrients
Carbon Dioxide	Water	Chlorophyll	Oxygen

REACTANTS ——— PRODUCTS

$$6\ CO_2\ +\ 6\ H_2O\ \longrightarrow\ C_6H_{12}O_6\ +\ O_2$$

_____   _____   _____   _____

_____

Reading Strategy: SEQUENCE of EVENTS

Pages 254–255 of your textbook describe the carbon cycle. The carbon cycle illustrates how carbon is moved and recycled through our environment by both living and non-living things. Although each step is occurring at all times, the steps follow a general order or sequence. Identifying the sequence of steps in a process such as this can help you remember and understand what you read.

Below are several statements related to the carbon cycle. Number the steps to show their general sequence. The first one has been done for you.

_____ When fossil fuels are burned, carbon dioxide is released into the atmosphere.

_____ As organisms decompose, the carbon stored in their bodies is released into the soil, the atmosphere, or the water.

_____ The leftover remains of organisms may form coal and fossil fuels, such as oil.

_____ Consumers release carbon dioxide as a waste product after respiration.

_____ Producers and consumers die and begin to decompose.

___1___ Plants take in carbon dioxide and use it in photosynthesis to produce glucose and oxygen.

_____ Buried remains of organisms become fossilized underneath Earth's surface.

_____ Consumers take in the carbohydrates created by producers.

Apply what you learned to answer the Questions below.

1. Other than the methods listed above, describe three ways carbon might be released into

   the atmosphere. _____

   _____

2. How is carbon dioxide in the ocean used by organisms such as clams, oysters, and corals?

   _____

   _____

Elaborate

Visual Literacy: Reading Images

Throughout the Elaborate section of your textbook, you are asked to interpret many satellite images. Satellite images are pictures of Earth that have been created from data detected by satellites. They help us see what is occurring over large areas of land or water, and give us information about Earth that is sometimes hard to detect from Earth's surface.

When you look at an image, be sure to read the captions that accompany it. Then, look at legends or keys that explain details within the image.

Look at Figure 13.23 on Page 256 of your textbook as you answer the Questions below.

1. What does this image show? _____

    _____

2. At the bottom of the image is a color bar. This is the key that tells us what the colors on the image mean. According to the bar:

    *   What is the unit that chlorophyll concentration

        is being measured in? _____

        Note: This means there is a milligram of chlorophyll (or more or less) in every cubic meter along the sea surface. This is a very small amount.

    *   What color shows the lowest chlorophyll concentration? _____

    *   What color represents the highest concentration? _____

3. Although chlorophyll is green in color, the green areas on this map do not represent the areas with the highest chlorophyll concentrations. What do the green areas show?

    _____

    _____

4. The gray area in this image represents land. Does the shape of the gray look familiar to you? It should! This is North America. You can also see Central America, the Caribbean, and the very top of South America. Find the area of chlorophyll that is shown inside the United States. Why does this appear? What is located there?

    _____

    _____

5. Which areas have the highest concentration of chlorophyll, and therefore phytoplankton? What might this mean?

_____

_____

6. In your text, you are told that the Black-footed Albatross population is often found along coastlines in California. Why do you think this bird population might frequent this area?

_____

_____

_____

7. How might development and pollution along coastlines affect phytoplankton populations?

_____

_____

Reading Strategy: CAUSE and EFFECT

You are reading about algal blooms and their causes and effects. Remember, a cause is the reason that something happens. An effect is what happens as a result. An algal bloom is an increase in the amount of phytoplankton in an area. Satellites help us determine where algal blooms are occurring by detecting concentrations of the green pigment chlorophyll. When an algal bloom occurs, and the phytoplankton population increases, chlorophyll concentrations also increase.

There are two main causes of algal blooms. Use Pages 256 and 258 to help you find the two causes of algal blooms and answer the Questions below.

1. What are the natural causes of an algal bloom? _____

_____

_____

2. How can human activities cause algal blooms? _____

_____

_____

Name _____ Class _____ Date _____

Following is a Cause and Effect diagram. Use Pages 256 and 258 of your textbook and your knowledge of marine science to record the harmful effects of algal blooms in the circles of the chart.

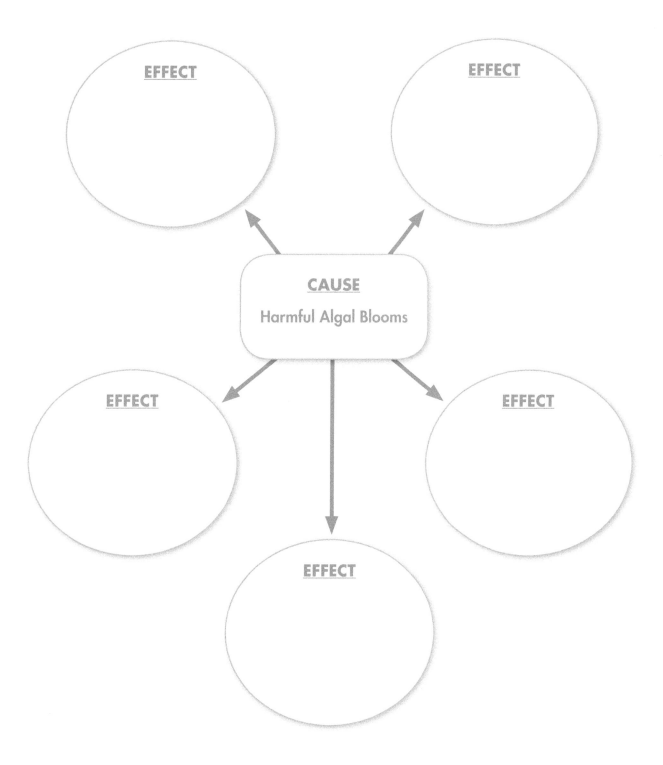

EFFECT

EFFECT

CAUSE

Harmful Algal Blooms

EFFECT

EFFECT

EFFECT

Evaluate

Lesson Summary

- Microscopic organisms such as phytoplankton, which live in the ocean, use the Sun's energy to conduct the chemical process of photosynthesis.

- Phytoplankton use nutrients, carbon dioxide, and water in the ocean for this process.

- Photosynthesis results in the creation of oxygen, which is released into the atmosphere, and glucose, which is stored as energy and used by consumers in the food web.

- Some of the oxygen produced during photosynthesis forms the ozone layer that protects us from the Sun's harmful radiation.

- Carbon is cycled through the environment by both non-living and living things.

- Carbon dioxide is used by plants during photosynthesis and is released by animals during respiration.

- Carbon can be introduced into the environment through natural means such as respiration, decomposition, forest fires, and the eruption of volcanoes.

- Carbon can also be released through human activities such as the burning of fossil fuels, agriculture, mining, and deforestation.

- We can use satellite images to see chlorophyll concentrations. This helps us determine where phytoplankton populations are and also enables us to track marine animals.

- Algal blooms can occur naturally when nutrients and light are readily available or as a result of human activities when sewer runoff or agricultural waste enters the water.

- Algal blooms, which can be seen by satellite imagery, can have harmful side effects to people and marine organisms.

Lesson Review

Review key concepts of the Lesson by turning to the anticipation guide that you started at the beginning of the Lesson. Review each statement again. Decide if you still agree with your original answer, or if you would like to change your response. In the Explanation column, write a one-sentence reason explaining why the statement is true or changing the statement so that it is correct.

Organize Your Thoughts

On Page 261 of your textbook, you are asked to create a multimedia presentation, a poster, or an essay to demonstrate your knowledge and comprehension of the carbon cycle. Use the Questions and chart below to help you organize your thoughts and arrange your information before working on your project.

Question	Answer
Why is the carbon cycle so important?	
What are three forms in which carbon exists?	
How do plants use carbon?	
How do animals use carbon?	
How does carbon enter the atmosphere?	
How does carbon leave the atmosphere?	
How does carbon enter the biosphere?	

Question	Answer
How does carbon leave the biosphere?	
How does carbon enter the hydrosphere?	
How does carbon leave the hydrosphere?	
How does carbon enter the lithosphere?	
How does carbon leave the lithosphere?	
What human activities release carbon into the atmosphere?	
What role do fossil fuels play in the exchange of carbon?	
Where does most of Earth's carbon exist?	

Name _____ Class _____ Date _____

14 Biodiversity in the Ocean

BIGIDEAS

- Oceans support thriving communities of organisms that depend on each other for survival.

- Organisms can be classified into groups according to their characteristics and behaviors.

Engage

Lesson Preview

Before reading and trying the activities in your textbook, survey the Lesson by scanning the headings, images, captions, and bold terms. Record what you predict the Lesson will be about in the first row of the chart below. Then, record questions that arose from scanning the Lesson in the second row. As you read, record in the third row of the chart the answers to your questions. Later, you will record a short summary of the Lesson.

Predictions	
Questions	
Answers	
Summary	

Vocabulary Review

Complete the chart below as you read Pages 264–265 of your textbook. Write the definition of each vocabulary term in your own words. Then, write a note to yourself on how you can remember the meaning of each term. Use the chart to review key concepts after you have finished the Lesson.

Term	Definition	How I Will Remember
Biodiversity		
Population		
Genetic diversity		
Plankton		
Nekton		

Explore

Build Concept Vocabulary

Before trying the activities in the Explore section of your textbook, use the concept web below to build your understanding of key concept vocabulary. The center and inner circles have been completed with criteria for classifying organisms. Record in the outer circles categories of each criteria along with a definition and example for each.

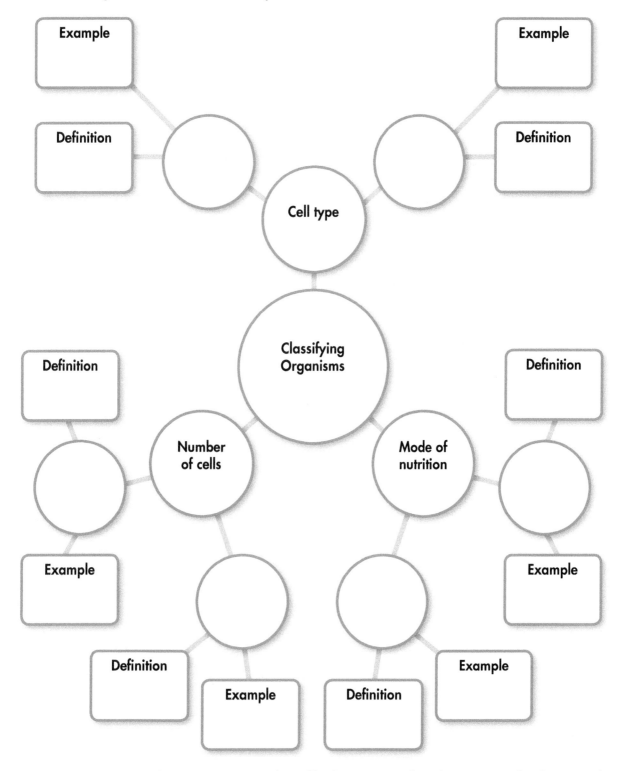

Practice Process Skills: MAKE OBSERVATIONS

The Cyberlab on Pages 266–267 of your textbook ask you to make observations about plankton. Remember that making observations is a key skill in the process of scientific inquiry. When we make observations we use our senses to take in information about our world.

Before conducting the Cyberlab described in your textbook, practice making observations with the following activity. Look at the picture below. Describe the picture with as many details as possible in the spaces provided.

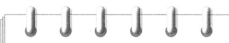

Scientists often use tools to extend their senses and make more detailed observations. For the Cyberlab in your textbook, you will use a microscope. Microscopes enlarge objects and help us see tiny organisms, items, or details that are hard to detect with the eye alone.

1. _____

   _____

2. _____

   _____

3. _____

   _____

4. _____

   _____

5. _____

   _____

6. _____

   _____

Credit: photos.com

7. _____

8. _____

Recall that data from observations can be quantitative or qualitative. Quantitative data involve numbers or measurements of things. Qualitative data include physical, unmeasured descriptions.

Classify the following observations as quantitative or qualitative by placing a check mark in the appropriate column. When you have finished, go back and classify the observations you made about the picture as quantitative or qualitative.

Observation	Qualitative	Quantitative
Five seagulls perched on the buoy.		
A colorful kite flew in the sky.		
The waves were strong as they crashed against the shore.		
The temperature of the water was 23 °C.		
The wind blew north at 20 kilometers per hour.		

Explain

Vocabulary Review

As you read Pages 268–274 of your textbook, define each vocabulary term in your own words. Then, write yourself a note that will help you remember the meaning of each term.

Term	Definition	How I Will Remember
Taxonomy		

Term	Definition	How I Will Remember
Binomial nomenclature		
Hierarchy		
Invertebrates		
Fertilization		
Chemosynthesis		

Term	Definition	How I Will Remember
Halophile		
Methanogen		
Thermophile		
Common ancestor		

Practice Process Skills: RECORD DATA

Page 270 of your textbook asks you to complete a data table using text that you will read. Scientists often organize data into simple tables to make it easier to review and analyze information. Before completing a data table, it is always important to review the information and headings in the first column and row of the chart or table.

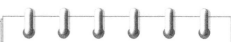

Keep in mind that it is acceptable to fill in the chart out of order. You will likely be able to fill in some of the answers right away based on your prior knowledge. For other questions you will need to find the answers in the written descriptions of the kingdoms or in other resources.

Look at the data table in your textbook and answer the Questions below to help you get started with the activity.

1. Read each Question in the data table on Page 270. You will record the answers to these Questions for each kingdom in your data table. Using your own words, what information will you need to record in each row of the table?

   a. _____

   b. _____

   c. _____

   d. _____

   e. _____

   f. _____

Now practice answering the table Questions for the Kingdom Animalia.

2. Are animals unicellular or multicellular?

   Hint: Humans are animals.

   _____

3. Are animals autotrophs or heterotrophs—do they produce their own food?

   _____

4. Are animals eukaryotic or prokaryotic—do they have a nucleus in their cells?

   _____

5. Think about the structures of animal cells. What are some organelles that you find in the cells of animals?

   _____

6. Finally, it is time to list some examples. What are three examples of land-based animals? What are three examples of marine animals?

   Land Animals   **Marine Animals**

   a. _____   a. _____

   b. _____   b. _____

   c. _____   c. _____

You have answered Questions about a Kingdom that you are familiar with, Animalia. Now practice finding answers in the text to complete the data table for the Protista Kingdom. Use the text about Protista on Page 272 of your textbook to answer the Questions below. Then, apply what you learned to complete the data table on Page 270.

1. Read the first paragraph. What information does it supply?

   _____

   _____

2. Read the first sentence of the second paragraph. What information does it supply?

   _____

   _____

3. Now it is time to search for information about the number of cells and cell structures. What do the two paragraphs say?

   _____

   _____

4. Now scan the two paragraphs and images again. Can you find any examples of marine protists? How about land or freshwater protists?

   _____

   _____

Elaborate

Review What You Learned

After completing the Local Plankton Exploration lab described on Pages 279–282 of your textbook, answer the following Questions to review what you learned.

5. Describe the experience of making your own scientific tools. What was interesting, difficult, or surprising about making the plankton net?

_____

_____

_____

_____

_____

_____

_____

6. Describe the experience of collecting your own scientific samples. What was interesting, difficult, or surprising about collecting the plankton samples?

_____

_____

_____

_____

_____

_____

_____

_____

7. When you observed the plankton samples under the microscope, what did you find most interesting, difficult, or surprising?

_____

_____

_____

_____

_____

_____

_____

8. How did the organisms you collected in your local environment compare to those seen on the DVD?

_____

_____

_____

_____

_____

_____

_____

Evaluate

Lesson Summary

- Oceans support a diversity of life. Diversity describes not only different types of organisms, but differences from organism to organism within a species.

- Ecosystems thrive with higher levels of biodiversity.

- Plankton are biologically diverse organisms that depend on the movement of water for travel.

- Organisms are classified biologically with a science called taxonomy.

- Organisms are connected in an evolutionary manner to their common ancestors through the Tree of Life.

- Organisms have structures that enable them to carry out life processes and meet survival requirements.

- An organism's structures supports its functions.

Lesson Review

Return to the chart on Page 145 of this workbook that you started at the beginning of this Lesson. Retell the key concepts of the Lesson in your own words. To help organize your thoughts, use the graphic organizer below.

Important Idea	Important Idea	Important Idea	Important Idea

Summary

15 Marine Populations

BIGIDEAS

- Marine populations shift over time as a result of natural and human-made changes. Both biotic and abiotic factors in an ecosystem can cause populations to increase or decrease.

- Some populations are able to cope with changes, while others may become endangered if select factors in their environments do not become more favorable.

- The Endangered Species Act was developed to protect populations of organisms.

Engage

Activate Prior Knowledge

In this Lesson you will learn about populations in marine ecosystems and will examine three different marine species. Think about the marine species in the ecosystems around your home. You may not live near an ocean, but find a water habitat near you, such as a pond, lake, or stream. Observe the ecosystem and list the organisms you see there.

Organisms in Water Ecosystems Near My Home	

Once you have made your list, choose one of the organisms and write what you know about it. If possible, include information about what it eats and other places it lives in your state. Write a paragraph about the organism below. Share your paragraph with a partner.

_____

_____

_____

_____

Visual Literacy: Reading Graphs

Throughout this Lesson, you will find a variety of graphs. Remember, graphs show information in a visual way and help you see patterns or relationships in data quickly. Knowing how to read different kinds of graphs is an important skill. Here is how some graphs are used:

- A line graph, such as on Pages 286, 289, and 291 of your textbook, is used to compare two factors, or **variables**. Line graphs are often used to show changes over time.

- A bar graph, such as on Pages 293 and 299, shows numbers or values of things. Bar graphs can be horizontal or vertical. The ones on Pages 293 and 299 are *double* bar graphs. They show two related sets of data on one graph.

Look at the data table and graph below for the total numbers of manatees seen in January aerial surveys along both Florida coasts. Note: This does not provide population estimates. Then, answer the Questions that follow to review your graph reading skills.

Florida Manatee

Quantity Seen	Year
1,900	2000
3,300	2001
3,000	2003
3,100	2005
2,800	2007
3,800	2009
5,100	2010
4,800	2011

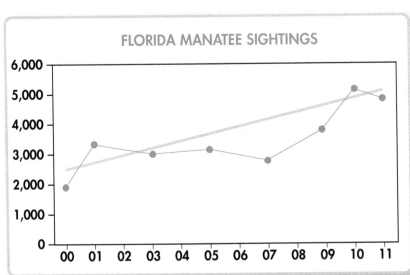

Credit: Adapted from Florida Fish and Wildlife Conservation Commission

1. What is the overall trend in the Florida Manatee sightings between 2000 and 2011?

_____

_____

2. By how many animals have the sightings increased from January 2001 to January 2009?

_____

3. What is the percent increase in manatee sightings from 2000 to 2011?

_____

_____

Explore

Review What You Learned

After completing the activity on Page 287 of your textbook, answer the Questions below to review what you learned about each animal species.

1. In what ecosystems can the Florida Manatee be found? What is its natural range?

   _____

   _____

   _____

2. What are some features of the Florida Manatee? Describe how it looks, what it eats, and how quickly or slowly it reproduces.

   _____

   _____

   _____

3. What are some possible threats to manatees?

   _____

   _____

   _____

4. In what ecosystems can the Green Sea Turtle be found? What is its natural range?

   _____

   _____

   _____

5. What are some features of the Green Sea Turtle? Describe how it looks, what it eats, and how quickly or slowly it reproduces.

_____

_____

_____

_____

6. What are some possible threats to sea turtles?

_____

_____

_____

7. In what ecosystems can the Common Dolphinfish be found? What is its natural range?

_____

_____

_____

8. What are some features of Common Dolphinfish? Describe how it looks, what it eats, and how quickly or slowly it reproduces.

_____

_____

_____

_____

9. What are some possible threats to Common Dolphinfish?

_____

_____

_____

Explain

Vocabulary Review

Complete the chart below as you read Pages 291–295 of your textbook. Write the definition of each vocabulary term in your own words. Then, write a note to yourself on how you can remember the meaning of each term. Use the chart to review key concepts after you have finished the Lesson.

Term	Definition	How I Will Remember
Population		
Population dynamics		
Carrying capacity		
Population density		

Review What You Learned

After reading the Explain section of your textbook, complete the activities and answer the Questions below to review what you learned. Classify the factors in the chart below as biotic or abiotic factors, and tell whether the factor tends to increase or decrease population size.

Factor	Abiotic or Biotic?	Affect on Population Size?
Polluted water		
Limited food sources		
Appropriate seasonal temperatures		
Unexpected climate change		
Addition of nutrients to the water		
Diversity within a species		
A new disease is introduced to an area		
Salt water leaks into a freshwater environment changing its salinity		

*On Pages 291–295 of your textbook you learned about clumped, uniform, and random population densities. For Questions 1–4, classify each description of a marine population as **clumped, uniform, or random.***

1. Fish that move in schools _____

2. Oyster larvae that settle on the seafloor in an unpredictable pattern _____

3. Distribution of organisms that are evenly spaced, such as some individual

   polyps _____

4. Animals that congregate near warm water areas in winter _____

Draw each type of population density below.

  clumped   **random**   **uniform**

Think about the effect of random, uniform, and clumped densities on the populations in an ecosystem. Then, answer Questions 5–7 in your own words.

5. Which kind of population density would be most susceptible to disease? Why?

   _____

   _____

6. Which kind of population density would be most difficult to protect? Why?

   _____

   _____

7. Which kind of population would be most susceptible to predators? Why?

   _____

   _____

Elaborate

The Elaborate section of your textbook discusses endangered organisms and laws that protect them. Use Pages 296 and 297 of your textbook to help you complete the following activities about this topic.

In the chart below, list three reasons why it is important to protect biodiversity in our ecosystems.

Important Reasons for Protecting Biodiversity

Explain the differences between the following terms:

Listed: _____

_____

Endangered: _____

_____

Threatened: _____

_____

Answer the following Question.

1. What does it mean when an organism is *de-listed* and how does this happen? _____

_____

_____

_____

_____

Reflect on Your Reading

On Pages 296–297 of your textbook you learned that people have differing opinions about how to treat the problem of endangered animals on Earth. Many biologists believe that humans are responsible for caring for endangered species because many of our human activities have led to organisms becoming extinct. Others believe that nature should be allowed to take its course when animals become endangered.

Use the scale below to record benefits and problems associated with protecting animals or letting nature take its course. Then, write your opinion on this issue.

The Issue:

Benefits	Problems

Organize Your Thoughts

Page 298 of your textbook asks you to prepare a presentation about an endangered species. To prepare for your presentation, do as much research as possible. The *Marine Science: The Dynamic Ocean* website will help you to choose a species. Then, use Internet resources and your school or local library to do further research. Your presentation will go more smoothly if you have ample information to share.

Record the information you find about your species in the concept map below. Then, use this map to organize your thoughts and prepare your presentation.

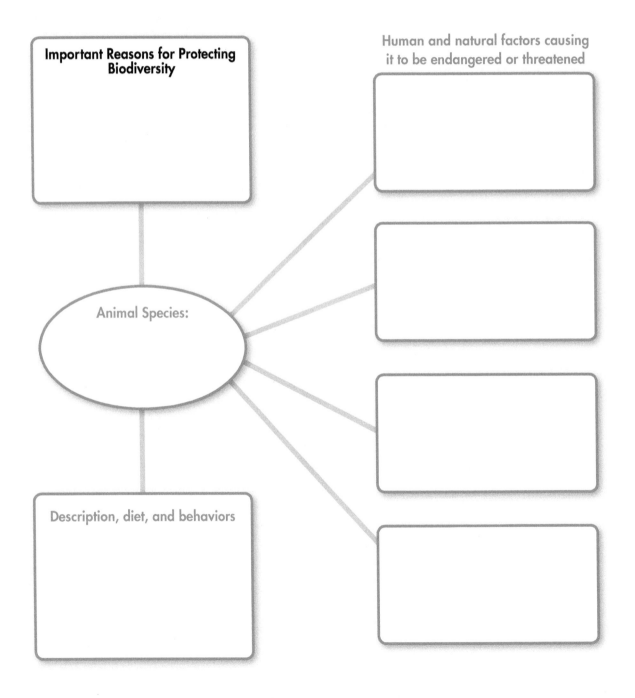

Important Reasons for Protecting Biodiversity

Human and natural factors causing it to be endangered or threatened

Animal Species:

Description, diet, and behaviors

Evaluate

Lesson Summary

- The populations of marine ecosystems change over time.

- Biotic and abiotic factors contribute to the increase or decrease of a population.

- Food supply, water temperature, salinity, light, nutrients, and space to move all affect the population dynamics and the carrying capacity of a population.

- Populations are distributed among their environments in various ways. Clumped, uniform, and random population patterns are common in marine ecosystems.

- Human activities can contribute to decreasing populations through fishing, pollution, and accidents with boats. Human activities can also contribute to increasing population through conservation efforts and passing of laws to limit fishing and boat use in marine ecosystems.

- The Endangered Species Act was created to protect threatened and endangered organisms. A population can be listed as endangered if it is in danger of extinction throughout most of its range. A population can be listed as threatened if it may become endangered in the near future.

Lesson Review

Answer the Questions below about the contents of this Lesson. Use your textbook, notes, and previous workbook pages to help you answer the Questions listed here.

1. What is one way that humans can protect the Florida population of Green Sea Turtles?

   _____

   _____

   _____

   _____

2. What may happen to a species if it exceeds its carrying capacity? _____

   _____

   _____

   _____

3. Describe three types of population densities often found in marine ecosystems.

_____

_____

_____

_____

4. How can we help keep a threatened species from becoming endangered?

_____

_____

_____

_____

5. What can you infer from reading a line graph that shows the population of Green Sea Turtles increasing year after year?

_____

_____

_____

_____

6. What are some abiotic factors that can decrease the growth of a marine population?

_____

_____

_____

_____

16 Population Changes

BIGIDEAS

- Genetic variations occur randomly in all organisms through mutations, and are not all beneficial to individual organisms.

- Evolution is a process in which the traits of organisms change over many generations. Evolution is influenced by natural selection.

- Adaptations help organisms to survive in their ecosystem.

Engage

Activate Prior Knowledge

In this Lesson, you will learn about change that occurs randomly in organisms over time called "genetic variation." Many of these variations occur as physical traits that can be seen easily. In marine animals, such traits may include patterns, colors, sizes, and body shapes. Variations may also include behavioral traits that are not as easily seen among individuals, such as speed and efficiency at finding food.

Before reading and trying the activities in your textbook, notice variations in the visible and behavioral traits of your classmates and complete the chart below.

What are some visible traits that vary among your classmates?	What are some behavioral traits that vary among your classmates?

Why do you think the traits among your classmates are so different?

Explore

Math Mini-Lesson

For the Explore activity on Pages 303–305 of your textbook, you will model genetic variations in sea stars. One step of the activity asks you to calculate the percentage of a particular variety of sea star compared to the whole population of sea stars. Remember that percentages are ways to show parts of a whole.

Before trying the activity in your textbook, review how to calculate percentages with the formula below and the example and Questions that follow.

$$\% = \frac{\text{portion of a set}}{\text{total set}} \times 100$$

Here's an example. Suppose you had a collection of 25 songs. Eight of the songs are pop songs, five of the songs are rap songs, and 12 of the songs are R&B songs. You could find the percentage of each type of song you have. Here's how you find the percentage of R&B songs:

Step 1: Insert the correct numbers into the formula.

$$\% \text{ of R\&B songs} = \frac{12 \text{ R\&B songs}}{25 \text{ songs}} \times 100$$

Step 2: Divide the number of R&B songs by the total number of songs.

$$12 \div 25 = 0.48$$

Step 3: Multiply the number you calculated above by 100 to calculate percentage of R&B songs.

$$0.48 \times 100 = 48\%$$

1. Using the information above, calculate the percentage of rap songs. Show your work.

2. Calculate the percentage of pop songs. Show your work.

Practice Process Skills: CONSTRUCT GRAPHS

You know that scientists often use graphs and tables to record or display data. Tables and graphs help show data in a visual and organized way so that it can be analyzed easily. Recall from Lesson 15 that a bar graph is one type of graph that scientists use. A bar graph shows amounts or values of things with rectangular boxes, or bars. Bar graphs are often used to show data about a single variable, such as population size.

Bar graphs have these key features:

- Show amounts or values with rectangular bars.

- Show values along one side of the graph.

- Have a title and labeled axes.

Look at the bar graph below and answer the Questions that follow to review making and reading bar graphs.

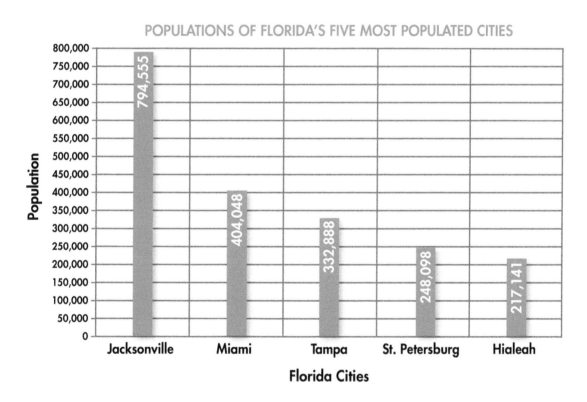

POPULATIONS OF FLORIDA'S FIVE MOST POPULATED CITIES

1. Which city has the 4th largest population? _____

2. About how much greater is the population of St. Petersburg than the population of

   Hialeah? _____

Below, create a bar graph showing the percentages of songs you calculated in the previous activity. Create labels and intervals.

TITLE: _____

Name Class Date

Explain

Vocabulary Review

Complete the chart below as you read Pages 305–313 of your textbook. Write the definition of each vocabulary term in your own words. Then, write a note to yourself on how you can remember the meaning of each term. Use the chart to review key concepts after you have finished the Lesson.

Term	Definition	How I Will Remember
Evolve		
Antibiotic resistance		
Natural selection		
Theory of Evolution		
Fossil record		
Transitional species		

Term	Definition	How I Will Remember
Extinct species		
Homologous structures		
Mutation		
Fitness		
Variations		
Adaptation		
Speciation		

Reading Strategy: TAKING NOTES

Taking notes as you read is an important tool that can help you remember key concepts. Outlining is one method for taking notes. When you outline, you show the major headings of a reading selection and then record definitions, a short summary, or a list of the main ideas of each section.

On Pages 310–313 of your textbook, you will read about factors Darwin described as part of his Theory of Evolution. Use the table below to outline these pages as you read. First record the section heads. Then, list the key points of each.

Section Title	What the Section Was About
I. Overproduction	
II.	
III.	
IV.	
V.	
VI.	

Elaborate

Reading Strategy: TAKING NOTES

Concept maps are another tool you can use for taking notes about a topic. In a concept map, such as the one shown below, you can record definitions, details, and examples related to a topic or concept.

Pages 313–315 of your textbook discuss invasive species and their effect on ecosystems. Use the concept map below to record key ideas and details about this topic as you read.

What is it (definition)?

Why are invasive species destructive?

MAIN CONCEPT

Invasive Species

What are some examples?

Organize Your Thoughts

The Extension Activity on Page 316 of your textbook asks you to research and write about an invasive species found in your area. Use the table below to organize your research and thoughts before creating your final product. Then, use the information in the table to write your brochure.

Questions	Answers
What is the invasive species?	
Where is its natural habitat?	
What is it like? Describe how it looks, what it eats, and what its natural predators are.	
How was this species introduced into your area?	
What effect does it have on local organisms or ecosystems?	
Why should people be concerned about this species?	
How can we help reduce the damage caused by this organism?	

Evaluate

Lesson Summary

- The Theory of Evolution, first described by Charles Darwin, explains that all species gradually change or evolve over many generations.

- Organisms that are better suited to compete for resources pass on their traits to their offspring in a process called natural selection. Organisms that are not able to compete die out.

- Natural selection is explained in the Theory of Evolution and is supported by evidence such as fossil records, body structures, and other observable traits.

- Scientists today can determine if organisms are closely related by identifying DNA sequences.

- A slight change in DNA is called a mutation and occurs randomly. Mutations lead to differences, or variations, within a species.

- Genetic traits that benefit an organism's survival and reproduction are called adaptations. These include both visible traits (or traits of appearance) and behavioral traits.

- The "survival of the fittest" refers to those organisms that are best adapted to the environment and are most likely to survive and reproduce successfully.

- Speciation occurs when organisms within a species become isolated and change dramatically over a long period of time, forming a distinct species.

Lesson Review

After completing the Lesson, do the puzzle below to review key concepts. Complete each statement with the correct term. Then, copy the numbered letters into the corresponding squares on the next page to reveal a quotation from Charles Darwin.

1. This evolutionary process of _____ occurs when a new biological species is created.

___ ___ ___ ___ ___ ___ ___ ___ ___
      54   15 2   34   39

2. Darwin reasoned that _____ of offspring was necessary to ensure that there would be enough adults to continue a species.

___ ___ ___ ___ ___ ___ ___ ___ ___ ___ ___ ___ ___
    51   38

3. Individuals with favorable traits being more likely to survive and reproduce is _____.

    __ __ __ __ __ __ __ __ __ __ __ __ __ __
    62   60   19   59 6   37

4. The process in which species change over many generations is called _____.

    __ __ __ __ __ __ __ __
       3   45 65 10

5. Shared characteristics in organisms or _____ is a result of shared ancestry.

    __ __ __ __ __ __ __ __ __ __
       61   50

    __ __ __ __ __ __ __ __ __ __
       33   44 66 24

6. The natural evolutionary process by which organisms are best adapted to their

    environment is called _____.

    __ __ __ __ __ __ __ __ __ __ __
    68 41 14   40   25 70   20

    __ __ __ __ __ __ __
    74 31   4   58

7. _____ is the result of subtle differences in the genes of individuals.

    __ __ __ __ __ __ __ __ __
       52 29

8. While a _____ may be harmful, another may be beneficial and give an organism an
    advantage for survival.

    __ __ __ __ __ __ __ __
          32 56 17 75

9. A species that inhabits a given area or region is called a _____.

    __ __ __ __ __ __ __ __ __ __ __ __
       35   57   49   43

10. Charles Darwin observed many animal species in the _____.

    __ __ __ __ __ __ __ __ __ __ __ __ __
    30   28   22   7 67   55

11. The English naturalist, _____, wrote *On the Origin of Species.*

__ __ __ __ __ __ __ __ __ __ __ __ __
23   48   42   9   21

12. A _____ is extinct but may represent a link to modern species.

__ __ __ __ __ __ __ __ __ __ __
          47   73 11   16 63

__ __ __ __ __ __
  13   26   71

13. A species becomes _____ when the last existing member of that species dies.

__ __ __ __ __ __ __
         72 36

14. An introduced or _____ is a species that lives outside its native range.

__ __ __ __ __ __ __ __ __ __ __ __ __
1   53 5 27 46   69   12 18   8

15. A contest between organisms for territory or food is called _____.

__ __ __ __ __ __ __ __ __ __ __
          64   76

Solve the quote from Charles Darwin.

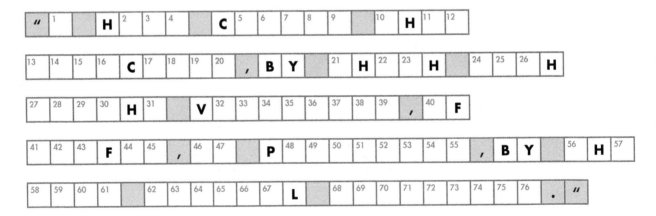

17 Food Webs in Action

BIGIDEAS

- A food web shows how energy and nutrients are exchanged between organisms within an ecosystem.

- Understanding food webs helps us to track animal movements and determine the impact of both natural and human-made events on specific ecosystems.

Engage

Activate Prior Knowledge

In this Lesson you will learn about food webs and the role they play in a healthy ecosystem. Use the chart below to record what you already know about these topics. After you complete the Lesson, use the chart to record new information you learned.

Before reading and trying the activities in your textbook, think about the Questions below. Record what you know about each topic in the What I Know column of the chart.

Question	What I Know	What I Learned
What is a food web?		
Why is the Sun important in marine ecosystems?		
How can humans affect food webs?		
Why is satellite imagery helpful to understanding food webs?		

Review What You Learned

The Engage section of your textbook discusses phytoplankton and marine animals. Phytoplankton are tiny ocean organisms that form the basis of many marine food webs. Organisms of all sizes depend on phytoplankton, or other organisms that eat phytoplankton, for nutrients and energy. As such, phytoplankton are a vital component of most marine ecosystems.

After reading Pages 320–321 of your textbook, answer the Questions below to review key concepts.

1. Because of their habits, North Atlantic Right Whales were hunted almost to extinction during the whaling era. What are some of the reasons they were hunted?

   _____

   _____

   _____

2. During the summer months, North Atlantic Right Whales can be found off New England coastlines. During the winter months, they can be found off the coast of Florida. Why might living in these habitats pose a danger to the species?

   _____

   _____

   _____

3. We use technology such as satellite imagery to track the location of phytoplankton blooms. Why do you think it is important to be able to do this?

   _____

   _____

   _____

4. How might marine pollution affect the North Atlantic Right Whale?

   _____

   _____

   _____

Explore

Build Background

The activity on Pages 322–323 of your textbook asks you to create a food web. The food web is a model or diagram that shows how energy and nutrients move through a community. The diagram below is an example. Each organism in this food web is connected to another by an arrow. The arrows show the direction of energy flow in the ecosystem. Fin whales eat zooplankton and get energy from zooplankton. This is represented in the diagram with an arrow that points from the zooplankton to the fin whale.

Study this food web and answer the Questions below to familiarize yourself with food webs before trying the **From Tiny to Tremendous: Marine Food Webs** *activity in your textbook.*

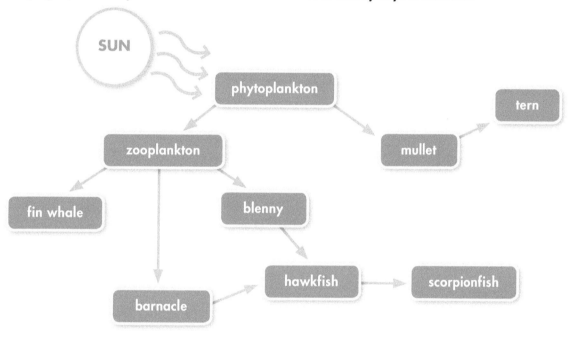

1. What is the initial source of energy for this food web? _____

2. Which organism in this food web is the producer? _____

3. Which organism in this food web is a top consumer? _____

4. If the blenny population in this ecosystem suddenly decreased, what changes might occur in the ecosystem?

   _____

   _____

Name ________________ Class ________ Date ________

Explain

Vocabulary Review

Complete the chart below as you read Pages 324–326 of your textbook. Write the definition of each vocabulary term in your own words. Then, write a note to yourself on how you can remember the meaning of each term. Use the chart to review key concepts after you have finished the Lesson.

Term	Definition	How I Will Remember
Producer		
Heterotroph		
Consumer		
Detritus		
Decomposer		

Term	Definition	How I Will Remember
Food web		
Trophic level		
Primary consumer		
Secondary consumer		
Tertiary consumer		
10% rule		

Use your textbook and completed vocabulary chart to answer the Questions below. For Questions 1–5, complete each statement with the correct vocabulary term.

1. Bacteria that make nutrients readily available to an ecosystem are called

    _____.

2. Lobsters and sharks are examples of _____ , which break down consumers after they die.

3. Snails and brittle stars are _____ that cannot move far;

    they feed on _____ that drifts down to the seafloor.

4. Organisms called _____ make up the first trophic level.

5. Jellyfish are examples of _____ that depend on mysids,

    or _____ , to provide them with energy and nutrients.

6. Other than zooplankton and pteropods, what are some examples of primary consumers?

    _____

    _____

7. How might an ecosystem change if all the bacteria and fungi died?

    _____

    _____

8. How do phytoplankton make their own food?

    _____

    _____

Reading Strategy: MAIN IDEA and DETAILS

When you read, it is important to understand the main idea of the passage you are reading. The *main idea* of a paragraph tells what the paragraph is "mainly", or mostly about. It is the key concept of the passage, or the most important idea being expressed. Often, but not always, the main idea is found at the beginning of a paragraph. Details help to support the main idea often by answering the questions who, what, where, when, why, how, or how many.

Below is a paragraph related to the Lesson you have been reading. Read the paragraph to locate the main idea and details.

> "The Right Whale was the first great whale to be hunted regularly by commercial whalers (from the 11th to the early 20th Century). Today, most right whale deaths are caused by human activities. Ships hit right whales accidentally because the whales rest, socialize, and feed near the surface in coastal areas where many ships travel. They also become entangled in fishing lines stretching hundreds of feet. Entanglement can keep the whales from eating, breathing, or swimming. Lines cutting into their skin can also cause fatal infections. The development and pollution of coastal marine habitats is another factor possibly affecting the recovery of the Northern Right Whale. The noise from ship traffic may also interfere with the whales' communication."

Credit: NOAA

What is the most important concept in the above paragraph?

This paragraph is **mainly** about how things that humans do can cause Right Whale deaths. If we read closely, we can see that the second sentence of the paragraph says, *"Today, most right whale deaths are caused by human activities."* So we know that this sentence provides us with the main idea of the paragraph.

Now let's look for some sentences that give us supporting details. Remember that details often answer a question about the main idea. For example, how do human activities cause Right Whale deaths?

Look at third sentence of the paragraph that says, *"Ships hit right whales accidentally because the whales rest, socialize, and feed near the surface in coastal areas where many ships travel."* This provides us with one detail about why many Right Whale deaths are caused by humans.

9. See if you can find two more details that support the main idea. _____

_____

_____

_____

_____

Note: Now that you know how to find the main idea and supporting details, use these skills as you read in your text.

Math Mini-Lesson

On Page 326 of your textbook, you are introduced to the 10% rule. The 10% rule states that, on average, only 10% of the available energy passes from one trophic level to the next. You learned that food is measured in calories; therefore, only 10% of the available calories are passed on from one organism to another.

Review calculating percents with the example and Questions below.

A percent is a portion or part of a whole. To find some percent of a number, you multiply the number by the percent, then divide the answer by 100. Here's an example. Suppose you wanted to find 10% of 20,000, you would solve the problem like this:

$(10 \times 20,000) \div 100 = ?$ Step 1: $10 \times 20,000 = 200,000$
Step 2: $200,000 \div 100 = 2,000$
10% of 20,000 is 2,000

If a producer had 20,000 calories of energy, only 2,000 of those calories would be available as energy to the primary consumer.

Use the above formula and Page 326 in your textbook to answer the following Questions.

1. If a secondary consumer had 3 million calories of energy, how many calories are

   available to the tertiary consumer? _____

2. If a producer had 200 million calories of energy, how many calories would be

   available to a secondary consumer? (*Read carefully!*) _____

3. If 250,000 calories are available to the primary consumer, how many are available

   to the secondary consumer? _____

4. If 30 million calories are available to the producer, how many calories are available

   to the tertiary consumer? _____

5. Why do you think all the energy from an organism cannot be passed on to the

   next trophic level? _____

   _____

   _____

Vocabulary Review

Use Pages 326–327 of your textbook to complete the Questions below. For Questions 1–6 match each term with the definition that best describes it.

1. ____ Proteins
   a. Main source of energy for organisms; may be simple or complex

2. ____ Vitamins
   b. Incorporated in body structures and provide energy; control chemical signals

3. ____ Minerals
   c. Store and transmit genetic information

4. ____ Carbohydrates
   d. Inorganic substances such as iron and zinc; required for processes such as transmitting nerve signals

5. ____ Nucleic acids
   e. Organic compounds necessary for metabolic processes

6. ____ Lipids
   f. Contain nitrogen; build an organism's body structures

For Questions 7–10, complete each sentence with the correct term from the word bank.

nutrient cycling	organic compounds	cellular respiration	nutrients

7. Vitamins, minerals, and water are three types of _____.

8. When decomposers break down waste and return the elements back to the soil and water,

   it is called _____.

9. Proteins, carbohydrates, and lipids are all examples of _____ because they contain hydrogen and carbon held together by covalent bonds.

10. _____ occurs when an organism breaks down food molecules to release stored energy.

Evaluate

Lesson Summary

- Food webs are an essential part of a healthy ecosystem.

- In a food web, a complex transfer of energy and nutrients occurs between organisms.

- Not all energy is passed on between levels of a food web.

- The cycling of nutrients, including nitrogen, is a necessary part of a functional ecosystem.

- Understanding relationships within food webs helps us to understand the health of ecosystems better and to track the movement of specific animal groups.

- Changes to an ecosystem can have an extensive impact on the health of that ecosystem as organisms are intricately linked within food webs.

- Both human activities and natural disruptions can have serious consequences for all organisms linked within a food web.

Lesson Review

Turn back to Page 163 of this workbook and record information you gained from the Lesson in the What I Learned column of the chart. Then, use this information as well as your notes and other workbook pages to write a summary of the Lesson in your own words.

Important Idea	Important Idea	Important Idea	Important Idea

Summary

18 Introduction to Marine Invertebrates

BIGIDEAS

- The majority of Earth's species are invertebrates.

- Invertebrates have a variety of characteristics, the most notable of which is the lack of a backbone.

- Different characteristics allow each species to fulfill specific niches in their ecosystem.

Engage

Activate Prior Knowledge

Below is an **anticipation guide**. On this anticipation guide you will see several statements that are related to what you will read about in this Lesson. Read each statement and make a mark in the box to show whether you agree with each statement or disagree with it. Use what you have learned in the previous Lessons to help you make your decisions. We will return to this anticipation guide after you have finished the Lesson to review your predictions and compare them with what you have learned.

Agree	Statement	Disagree
	To be classified as an animal, an organism must be able to move itself.	
	All animals are multicellular.	
	Amphibians and birds are classified in the same phylum.	
	Organisms such as sponges and coral are autotrophic.	
	Fish are invertebrates.	

Agree	Statement	Disagree
	Humans are more closely related to sea squirts than to lobster.	
	Jellyfish and sea urchins require water to live.	
	Many organisms in Kingdom Animalia are found only in the ocean.	
	Many organisms in an ecosystem may share the same niche, or job	
	Sea stars, roundworms, and snails are examples of invertebrate herbivores.	

Use your prior knowledge of the subject and what you have read in the Engage section of your text to help you answer the Questions below.

1. What characteristics do all *living things* share? _____

   _____

   _____

   _____

   _____

2. All animals are eukaryotic. What does this mean? _____

   _____

   _____

   _____

   _____

Explore

In this section of the textbook you are learning about the different phyla of invertebrates and the varied characteristics these organisms exhibit.

Use your text, the e-Tools from the classroom activity, and the diagrams you create in class to answer the Questions below.

1. Spiny-skinned organisms such as the sea urchin and sea star are classified as echinoderms. What interesting fact did you learn about the symmetry of these organisms as they age?

   _____

   _____

   _____

   _____

2. Phylum Arthropoda includes lobsters, crabs, and other organisms with jointed appendages and exoskeletons. Sea spiders and horseshoe crabs are classified in a specific subphylum. What is it called and what is the defining characteristic of this subphylum?

   _____

   _____

   _____

   _____

3. What are three ways that the worms in Phylum Annelida differ from the worms in Phyla Nematoda and Platyhelminthes?

   _____

   _____

   _____

   _____

4. Bivalves such as clams are part of Phylum Mollusca. However, unlike other mollusks, these organisms lack a certain part. What is the missing part called and what is its function?

_____

_____

_____

5. What does it mean to be hermaphroditic? Which phylum of worms is not typically hermaphroditic?

_____

_____

Fill in the fishbone chart below with the four defining characteristics of Phylum Chordata and then explain these characteristics. An example has been done for you.

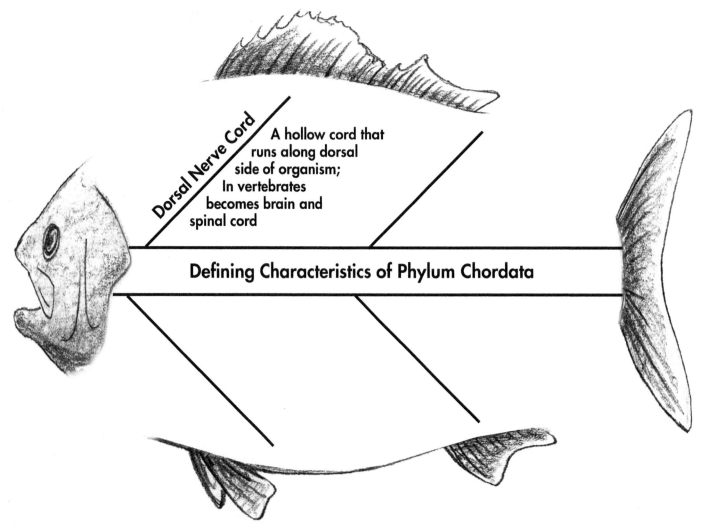

Dorsal Nerve Cord

A hollow cord that runs along dorsal side of organism; In vertebrates becomes brain and spinal cord

Defining Characteristics of Phylum Chordata

Explain

Vocabulary Review

Use Pages 346 through 350 in your text to help you complete the vocabulary activities below.

1. _____ morphology
   a. a species' job, or role, within an ecosystem

2. _____ physiology
   b. the study of the structures of organisms

3. _____ niche
   c. the study of the structures of organisms in the animal population

4. _____ anatomy
   d. the study of the processes within organisms

5. _____ substrate
   e. a surface on which an organism grows or is attached

Use your prior knowledge and the Explain section of the text to help you answer the Questions below.

6. Circle the ecosystem where food is more abundant:

   Kelp Forest   or   Open Ocean

   Deep Sea   or   Coral Reef

   Open Ocean   or   Salt Marsh

7. Name at least three places where adult marine invertebrates may be found.

   _____

   _____

   _____

   _____

   _____

In your text you read about the different methods organisms within the invertebrate phyla use to feed.

Below is a sea star diagram, which we will use as a type of graphic organizer to organize our thoughts and ideas about what we have learned to help us better understand this topic. In each ray or arm of the sea star, you will fill in one method of feeding, as well as, at least, two details about that method. An example has been done for you. Use your text to help you fill in the sea star.

SUSPENSION FEEDING
- Organisms rely on water currents to bring food to them.
- Organisms manipulate their arms and feet to capture food particles from the water currents to transfer them to their mouths and digestive systems.

Methods of Feeding Used by Invertebrates

The following paragraph is about the feeding methods of invertebrates, which you have just studied. Fill in the paragraph below with the missing terms from the word bank below. Use Pages 347–350 in your text and the sea star chart you created to help you complete this activity.

active filter feeders   carnivores   herbivores   excurrent siphon

detritus   evisceration   incurrent siphon

water vascular system   parapodia   predators

There are multiple ways in which invertebrates obtain the nutrients they need in order to

produce the energy necessary to complete their life's activities. Some organisms, such as the

sea urchin, are _____, which eat only plants, algae, and other vegetation.

Other organisms have a diet which consists of eating other animals. These organisms are

called _____, or _____. Predators such as the sandworm

use a fleshy extension called _____ to help them swim, or crawl through

sediment to search for prey and then grab it with their powerful jaws. Both herbivores and

carnivores are important members of an ecosystem. For example, herbivorous sea urchins eat

kelp, while predatory sea otters eat the sea urchins, in order to keep their population in check.

Another method of invertebrate feeding is known as filter feeding. Bivalves, such as clams,

are known as _____, pumping water in through an _____

_____ across their gills to gather oxygen and food. The clam then releases waste and

digested food through the _____, pushing water out of the organism.

Suspension feeders, such as crinoids, have a _____, sticky

water-filled tubes that capture food and transfer the particles to the mouth and digestive

system. Still other organisms feed on _____, or decomposing animal and

plant remains that fall to the seafloor. These deposit feeders are important because they

recycle nutrients, making them readily available to other organisms in the marine ecosystem.

Elaborate

Write the squid part names and part functions in the charts below.

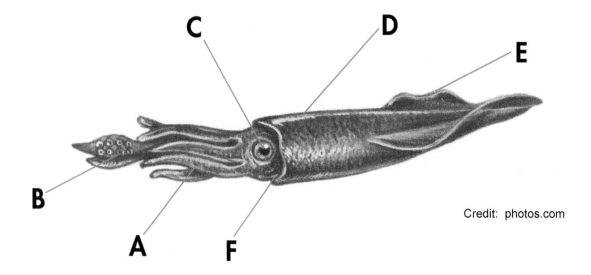

Credit: photos.com

Letter	Part Name	Function
A		
B		
C		
D		
E		

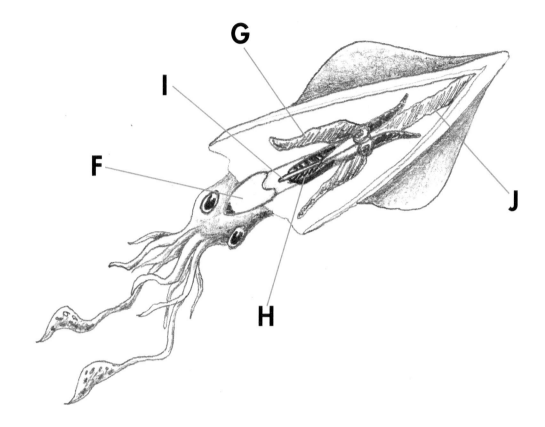

Letter	Part Name	Function
F		
G		
H		
I		
J		

Evaluate

You have read about many different phyla of invertebrates. Based on the information provided below, identify each organism and explain what phylum you would classify the animal in and why.

1. This organism is made up of a jelly-like substance, arranged in an umbrella-like shape. Tentacles hang off of the umbrella shape. There is a central mouth and a sac-like digestive system. _____

   _____

   _____

   _____

   _____

   _____

2. This organism exhibits a round cross-section and both sides of the body are nearly identical. _____

   _____

   _____

   _____

   _____

   _____

   _____

A **Venn diagram** is a graphic organizer that allows us to compare and contrast similarities and differences between two different items or ideas. In Lesson 18 you read about different phyla of invertebrates.

Use the text and your knowledge of the phyla to help you complete the Venn diagram on the next page. List four to five facts about each of the topics. Also, include at least two similarities that they have in the center section of the overlapping circles.

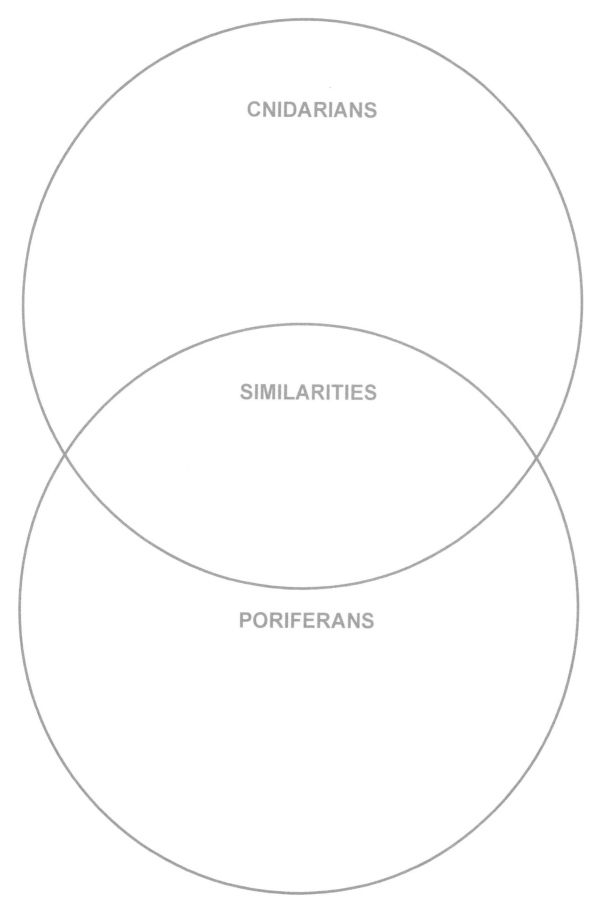

CNIDARIANS

SIMILARITIES

PORIFERANS

Answer the following Questions.

3. Give an example of how two species might have similar feeding habits, but still fulfill different niches. _____

_____

_____

_____

_____

_____

4. Explain what an Aristotle's Lantern is and describe its function. _____

_____

_____

_____

_____

_____

5. Explain the process of evisceration. Give an example of an organism that carries out this process. _____

_____

_____

_____

_____

_____

_____

Below is the same anticipation chart that you used in the beginning of the Lesson to make predictions about the topic. Now that you have read the Lesson, conducted experiments and read diagrams and charts about the topic, review each of the statements again. Decide if you still agree with your original answer, or if you would like to change your response. On the blank line below each statement, write a one-sentence reason proving why the statement is true, or changing the statement so that it is correct.

Agree	Statement	Disagree
	To be classified as an animal, an organism must be able to move itself.	
	All animals are multicellular.	
	Amphibians and birds are classified in the same phylum.	
	Organisms such as sponges and coral are autotrophic.	
	Fish are invertebrates.	

Agree	Statement	Disagree
	Humans are more closely related to sea squirts than to lobster.	
	Jellyfish and sea urchins require water to live.	
	Many organisms in Kingdom Animalia are found only in the ocean.	
	Many organisms in an ecosystem may share the same niche, or job	
	Sea stars, roundworms, and snails are examples of invertebrate herbivores.	

Lesson Summary

- Ninety-seven percent of animal species on Earth are invertebrates.

- Because invertebrates have such varied characteristics, there are many ways in which these organisms obtain nutrition.

- Invertebrates play an integral role in the marine ecosystem.

19 Biology of Fishes

- The majority of vertebrates are fish.

- There are several different classes of fish.

- Fish can be found in a wide variety of ecosystems.

- Fish and sharks have many adaptations which allow them to fulfill different niches in various marine ecosystems.

Engage

In this Lesson you will learn about the characteristics of various fish, and how they have adapted to their individual ecosystems.

Before you read the Lesson, read each Question below and think about what you already know about the topic. Write a few ideas, thoughts, or sentences in the What I Know column. After you complete the Lesson, you will visit an expanded chart to complete a What I Learned column using information you have discovered through reading the text and through the activities and experiments you have completed during this Lesson.

Question	What I Know
How do you know if an animal is a fish?	
What characteristics do fish exhibit?	
Where can fish be found?	

Question	What I Know
Why do different species of fish live in different ecosystems?	
How do fish breathe?	
What kind of things do fish eat?	
Can different species of fish occupy the same niche?	
How many classes of fish are there?	
How do these classes differ?	
How are sharks classified?	
What do you know about sharks? (where do they live/what do they eat, etc.)	

Use your prior knowledge and the Engage section of the text to help you answer the Questions below.

1. Approximately how long have fish existed in the ocean? _____

   _____

   _____

   _____

2. Many species of fish commonly travel in groups. What are groups of fish called? _____

   _____

   _____

   _____

Explore

Answer the Questions below.

1. Approximately how many species of fish exist? _____

   _____

   _____

   _____

2. What percentage of the ocean has been fully explored? _____

   _____

   _____

   _____

3. Give at least five examples of a marine ecosystem and/or freshwater body. _____

_____

_____

_____

_____

Explain

Answer the Questions below.

1. Describe the bodies of jawless fish. _____

_____

_____

_____

_____

2. How do jawless fish feed? What do they eat? _____

_____

_____

_____

_____

_____

Below is a diagram of a bony fish, similar to the one seen in your text. Match each letter in the chart to the corresponding part on the diagram. Then, explain each part's function. An example has been done for you.

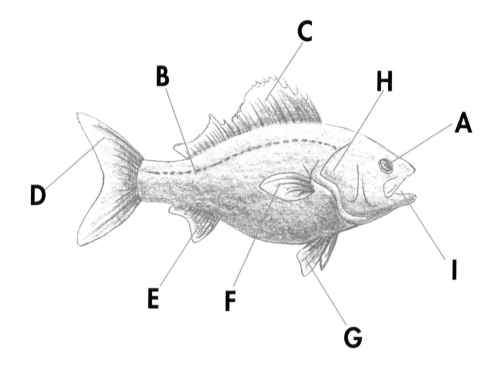

Letter	Part Name	Function
A	Eyes	Help fish to see while swimming and to spot prey
B		
C		
D		

Letter	Part Name	Function
E		
F		
G		
H		
I		

1. Where is the ventral side of a bony fish located?

   _____

   _____

2. What do the fins and scales of a bony fish typically look like? _____

   _____

   _____

   _____

3. Do all fish have exactly the same parts/structures? Why or why not? Give an example.

_____

_____

_____

_____

_____

_____

In this Lesson, you are reading about three classes of fish. The following paragraph is about cartilaginous fish. Use your text and the word bank to help you fill in the blanks to complete the paragraph below.

gill slits	dentin	nostrils	spiracles
cartilage	placoid scales	fossilized	

Cartilaginous fish is a class that includes sharks, skates, and rays and has existed on Earth for almost 450 million years. These fish do not have bones. Instead their skeletons are made up of _____, which is the same bony substance that makes up human noses and ears. Cartilage gives these fish flexibility, but teeth are often the only thing that is found _____ after the animal has decomposed. The teeth are not made of cartilage but of a hard substance called _____. These fish take in water through structures called _____, which are located on their heads. The water then passes over the gills and out through the _____. These fish must constantly swim in order to keep water flowing over their gills. Unlike bony fish, the scales of a cartilaginous fish feel rougher and will not flake off. These _____ are spiny and tooth-like. The _____ of these fish are used to enhance their sense of smell, rather than for breathing.

A **Venn diagram** is a graphic organizer that allows us to compare and contrast similarities and differences between two different items or ideas. In Lesson 19 you are reading about how various species of fish fulfill different niches in an ecosystem.

Use the text to help you complete the two Venn diagrams below. List two to four facts about each of the fish. Include at least two similarities that they have in the center section of the overlapping circles. Don't forget to use the pictures and captions in the text to help you find information for your diagrams.

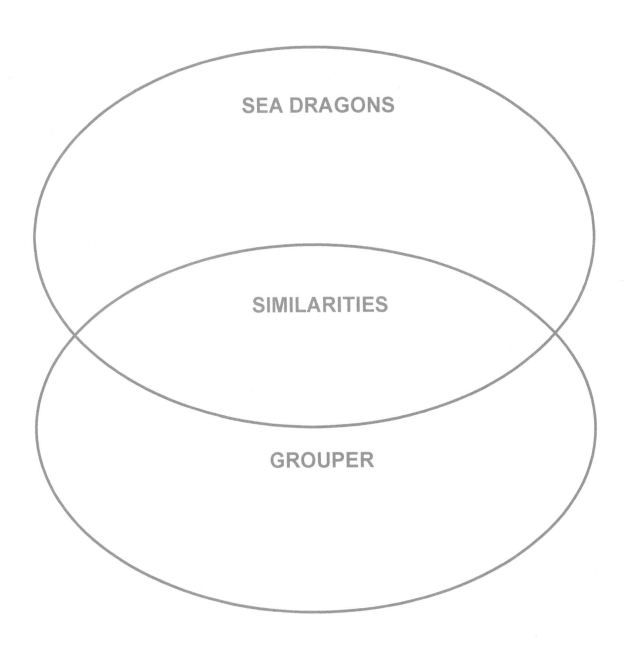

SEA DRAGONS

SIMILARITIES

GROUPER

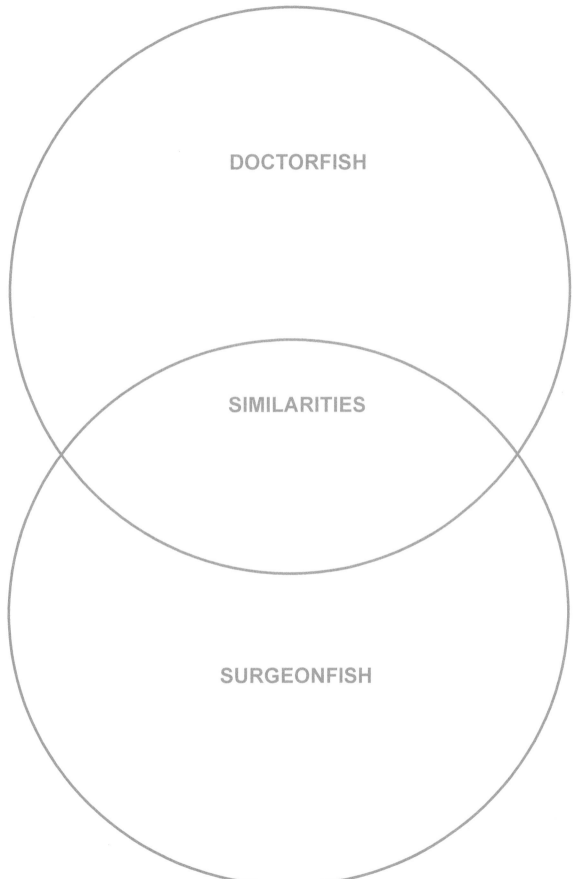

DOCTORFISH

SIMILARITIES

SURGEONFISH

When you read, it is important to understand the main idea of the passage you are reading. Remember that the **main idea** of a paragraph tells what the paragraph is "mainly", or mostly about. It is the key concept of the passage, or the most important idea being expressed. Often, but not always, the main idea is found at the beginning of a paragraph. **Details** help to support the main idea often by answering the questions who, what, where, when, why, how, or how many.

Below is a paragraph from your text. Read the paragraph to locate the main idea and details, and write them on the lines provided below.

> *"There are many niches within an ocean ecosystem to be filled. This is a good thing, because no two species can occupy the exact same niche at the same time and place; many niches provide opportunities for many animals. If the same niche were being filled by more than one species, the result would be competition between the two species until one outcompeted the other. If you examine the organisms in an ecosystem, it might appear that two species are occupying the same niche. Upon closer inspection, however, you will see this is not the case." (p. 370)*

What is the most important concept in the above paragraph (what is this paragraph mainly about)? If you read the paragraph closely, you will see that this paragraph is mainly about how niches in an ecosystem work.

1. Which sentence tells you what main topic of the paragraph is? _____

    _____

    _____

    _____

2. Now let's look for some sentences that give us supporting details. Remember that details

    often answer a question about the main idea. For example, why is it important that there

    are many niches in an ecosystem? _____

    _____

    _____

3. See if you can find two more details that support the main idea. Remember to look for

    ideas that answer questions about the main topic of marine debris. _____

    _____

_____

_____

_____

Note: Now that you know how to find the main idea and supporting details, use these skills as you read in your text.

Elaborate

Use Pages 371–372 of your textbook, as well as the Swell Shark Video, to complete the following activity. Tell whether each statement is true or false. If a statement is false, change a word or phrase to correct it and make it true. The first example is completed for you.

1. Many species of sharks attack humans.   _____

2. Sharks have anywhere from 6–20 rows of teeth.   _____

3. Most species of sharks have an excellent sense of smell.   _____

4. Sharks sense sound with organs called spiracles.   _____

5. The egg cases of some sharks and rays are called mermaid's purses. _____

6. Sharks' caudal fins provide the animal with lift.   _____

7. A shark's "sixth sense" is the ability to detect electrical impulses. _____

8. Swell Sharks get their name from their habitat, among waves called swells. _____

9. Horn Sharks are named for a sharp horn found on their backs. _____

10. Angel Sharks are typically observed swimming in the open ocean. _____

Evaluate

In this Lesson you learned about the characteristics of various fish, and how they have adapted to their individual ecosystems. Before you read the Lesson, you wrote your ideas, thoughts, or sentences in the What I Know column.

Now that you have completed the Lesson, revisit the chart at the beginning of the Lesson. Now fill in the What I Learned column using information you have discovered through reading the text and through the activities and experiments you have conducted during this Lesson.

Question	What I Know	What I Learned
How do you know if an animal is a fish?		
What characteristics do fish exhibit?		
Where can fish be found?		

Question	What I Know	What I Learned
Why do different species of fish live in different ecosystems?		
How do fish breathe?		
What kind of things do fish eat?		
Can different species of fish occupy the same niche?		
How many classes of fish are there?		
How do these classes differ?		
How are sharks classified?		
What do you know about sharks? (where do they live/what do they eat, etc.)		

Lesson Summary

- Today more than half of living vertebrates are fish.

- Fish are classified into three classes: jawless, bony, and cartilaginous.

- Fish can be found in a variety of freshwater and marine ecosystems.

- Different species of fish have different structural adaptations that help them fulfill their role, or niche, in the ecosystem.

- No two species of fish can occupy the same niche.

- Sharks are a type of cartilaginous fish.

- Sharks are excellent predators, but their numbers are on the decline due to human activities, pollution, and climate change.

20 Marine Reptiles and Birds

BIGIDEAS

- Reptiles and birds are both present in the marine environment.

- Many of these species have developed specific structural adaptations which allow them to rely on the ocean.

Engage

Activate Prior Knowledge

In Lesson 20 you will be reading about marine reptiles and birds. The Engage section of Lesson 20 includes many pictures of these animals with descriptive captions.

In the chart below you will use information from those captions. You must fill in the missing piece of information in each row. This might include the species' name, its habitat/location, or 1–2 interesting facts about the species. An example has been done for you.

Species Name	Where Species can be Found	Interesting Fact
Snowy Egret	North America	These are long-legged wetland birds that inhabit both fresh- and saltwater marshes.
Emperor Penguins		
	Atlantic Ocean/Great Lakes	

		This species of turtle was rescued with other sea turtles after the 2010 Deepwater Horizon oil spill.
Loggerhead Sea Turtle		
	Midway Atoll	
		The wing design of these seabirds allows them to soar distances and conserve energy.
Hawksbill Sea Turtle		

1. Describe the difference between a *marine bird* and a *seabird*. _____

    _____

    _____

    _____

    _____

2. What two similar structures can be seen in both birds and turtles? _____

    _____

    _____

Explore

Sooty Shearwater Tracking Map

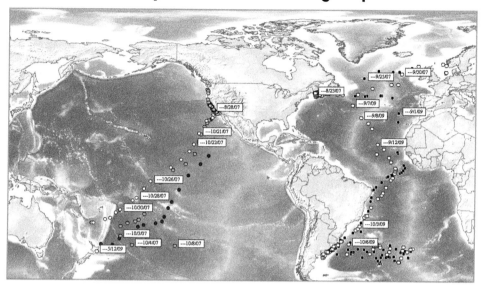

Credit: USGS/Western Research Center/Josh Adams

Sooty Shearwater Range Map

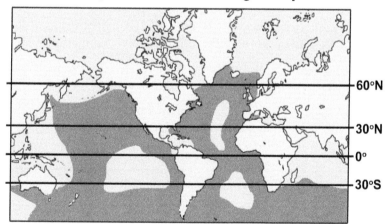

Credit: U.S. Satellite Laboratory

1. Compare and contrast the tracking map and the range map. What does each map show?

_____

_____

_____

_____

Explain

Vocabulary Review

Use Pages 384–388 in your text to help you complete the vocabulary activity below. Match each term with the correct definition.

1. _____ amniotic egg
2. _____ salt glands
3. _____ ectotherms
4. _____ amnion
5. _____ amphibians

a. a nourishing yolk sac used to feed the developing embryo

b. animals that live in water as juveniles, but must breathe air as adults

c. a reptilian egg containing a yolk sac

d. animals that depend on the external environment to moderate their internal temperature

e. special reptilian structures that secrete excess salt

Use your prior knowledge and the Explain section of the text to help you write the correct answer on the line.

6. Approximately how many years ago did reptiles evolve from amphibians? _____

_____

7. Name at least 3 common characteristics seen in reptiles. _____

_____

_____

_____

_____

8. Approximately how many species of reptiles exist? _____

9. How do reptilian salt glands work? _____

_____

_____

_____

10. Why do most reptiles live in warm climates? _____

_____

_____

_____

Use Pages 384–387 in your text to help you complete the chart below. For each species, list one adaptation that the species has developed, the purpose of that adaptation, the area where the species can be found, one interesting fact about the species, and something that puts the animal in danger, either from humans, or another environmental factor. One box has been filled in for each species to help guide you.

Species	Adaptation	Purpose of Adaptation	Habitat	Interesting Fact	Vulnerability of Species
Sea Snakes	Flat, stream-lined bodies, and a paddle-like tail				
Marine Lizards (Iguanas)			Galapagos Islands off coast of South America		
Saltwater Crocodiles					The population of the species has become endangered, mainly due to coastal development.

Name ____________________ Class ________ Date ________

In this Lesson you are learning about the features of certain species of Sea Turtles.

Use Pages 388–390 in your text to help you complete the bubble chart below. One example has been done for you in each bubble.

Characteristics of Sea Turtles

Adaptations

- Hard shell

Life Cycle

- eggs are laid in the sand

Diet

- jellyfish

Areas where they can be found

(Hint: refer to maps on pgs. 379–383)

- Large range

In this Lesson you are reading about a special species of turtle called the Leatherback Sea Turtle.

Below is a graphic organizer called a 5 W's and an H Chart. On this chart you will answer the Questions: Who, What, Where, When, Why, and How, filling in information about the Leatherback Sea Turtle from the text and class discussions.

Leatherback Sea Turtles	
Who are they?	
How big do they grow?	
Where are they found?	
What kind of adaptations do they have? (name at least 2)	
When do they release internal heat?	
Why has studying Leatherback Sea Turtles caused biologists to question what it means to be an ectotherm?	

Define the terms below in your own words.

Colonies _large groups of sea birds, sea birds gather together to breed_

_____

Preen _when sea birds clean their feathers; this helps species such as penguins spread oil throughout their layers, aiding water ponding_

Dynamic Soaring _technique is an ability some birds species have when they can lock out their wing joints an take advantage_

Match the pictures of various species of birds below with the correct description of that species. Use your text Pages 390–396 to help you.

_____   _____   _____   _____   _____

a. This seabird is identified by its bright red bill and long, stiff tail feathers and can dive over 100 meters.

b. This species of bird feeds almost exclusively at night.

c. This species of bird has a thin beak, perfect for picking out small crustaceans from the sand along the Gulf of Mexico.

d. These birds often travel thousands of miles, from the Northwest Hawaiian Islands to Alaska, to gather food for their chicks that remain at the nest.

e. This species breeds in the Midwest United States and relies on both salt- and freshwater environments.

Image credits (left to right): Meghan Marrero; U.S. Fish and Wildlife Service/John Foster; NOAA NESDIS, NODC/Mary Hollinger; National Science Foundation/Melissa Rider

Use Pages 390–396 in your text to help you answer the Questions below.

1. Compare and contrast the beaks of shorebirds and diving birds. _____

   Shorebirds beaks are longer and skinnier
   Sea birds beaks are thick
   _____
   _____

2. What do gulls feed on? _any food that humans drop._
   fish and freshwater invertebraes
   _____

3. What is the difference between a *seabird* and a *shorebird*? _____

   Seabirds have water proof plumage
   shorebirds have more feathers protecting their bodies
   _____

Circle the correct answer.

4. Which species has long, straw-like nostrils?

   a. Tubenoses   b. Penguins   c. Frigate Birds   d. Gulls

5. Antarctic penguins lay their eggs during the:

   a. Spring   b. Summer   c. Winter   d. Fall

6. Which birds' feathers are not very waterproof?

   a. Penguins   b. Frigate Birds   c. Tubenoses   d. Terns

7. Terns are the close relatives of which species of bird:

   a. Egrets   b. Pelicans   c. Gulls   d. Frigate Birds

Write true or false on the line next to each statement below. If the statement is false, explain why.

8. All birds can fly. _____

_____

9. All birds have feathers. _____

_____

10. All birds can control their own body temperature. _____

_____

11. Birds have dense, solid, bones. _____

_____

12. The majority of bird species live in and rely on the ocean. _____

_____

Elaborate

Sequencing helps us to list events in the order in which they occur. In Lesson 20, you read about the steps in the nesting cycle of sea turtles.

Below are the events that occur in this process. Write a number on the line next to each statement to arrange the steps in the correct order in which they happen, before the cycle begins again.

_____ During the spring and summer months, turtles mate just off the coast.

_____ Once incubated, the hatchling sea turtles emerge from the nest and scramble toward the water.

_____ Several weeks, or months later, the female turtle climbs up the beach and builds a nest in the sand.

_____ Female turtles lay eggs 3–5 times during the summer nesting season, with between 80-90 eggs in each nest.

_____ The female then deposits her eggs in the sand nest.

A **problem-solution chart** is an organizer that lists problems in one column and ways to fix those problems in the other column. It allows you to easily organize information about a particular topic. In your text, you are reading about the threats that sea turtles face. Several suggestions have been given as solutions to these problems.

Use the Elaborate section of your text, your class discussions, and your own ideas to fill in the boxes below. The first row has been completed as an example.

Problem	Solution
Light from beach communities disorients sea turtle hatchlings and prevents them from reaching the ocean.	Some communities have banned nighttime lights near the beach during nesting season.
Humans inadvertently walk on nests, disturbing, or killing eggs.	
	Many streetlights now use dim yellow bulbs.
Lights from hotels, office buildings, and homes cause sea turtle hatchlings to head in the wrong direction, leading them to get eaten by predators, run over by cars, or to dehydrate in the sun.	
FILL IN ONE OF YOUR OWN	

Evaluate

Lesson Review

You have now read all about marine reptiles and birds. You have read about the adaptations that those animals have developed to live in specific habitats, to find food, and to reproduce.

Think about all that you have learned and use the space below to write a postcard to a friend as you travel to one of the following places: the Gulf Coast, Hawaii, the Galapagos Islands, or the Atlantic Ocean and coastline. Use your textbook to help you determine which species of reptiles and birds live in these areas. Describe to your friend the species of marine reptile(s) and bird(s) you see on your trip, the adaptations these animals have, what they eat, and any other interesting facts about the species. Make sure to:

- Use vocabulary from the Lesson.
- Give at least one example of a marine reptile you have seen.
- Give at least one example of a marine bird you have seen.
- Describe the habitat of these species.

- Describe any adaptations these species have.
- Describe the diet of these species.
- Include one or two other interesting facts about the species you have chosen.
- Illustrate your postcard.

Lesson Summary

- There are a number of species of reptiles and birds that live in, or near the ocean.

- Many species of birds and reptiles have special structural adaptations that allow them to use the marine environment for breeding, to find food, or as their habitat.

- These marine reptiles and birds can be found all over the world from Antarctica to Alaska.

- These marine reptiles and birds migrate from warmer areas to colder areas and vice versa.

- Due to human activities, many of these species are threatened, or endangered.

21 Marine Mammals

BIG IDEAS

- There are many mammals that live in, or rely on, the ocean.

- Many of these marine mammals are quite large and rely on the density of water to accommodate their size.

- Researchers have many different ways of observing and studying these mammals.

- It is important that humans know how to correctly interact with not only marine mammals, but all animals.

Engage

Activate Prior Knowledge

Listed below are the names of various species, followed by a sample height/length and weight. The list includes land animals and marine mammals. Read through the list, then place the species in the correct order on the chart on the next page from lowest weight to greatest.

Wild Asian Water Buffalo 3.4m; 750kg

Polar Bear 2.6m; 400kg

Eastern Lowland Gorilla 1.8m; 225kg

West Indian Manatee 4.2m; 1,600kg

Humpback Whale 12m; 30,000kg

Red Kangaroo 2m; 100kg

Orca (Killer) Whale 6.7m; 5,500kg

Asian Elephant 3m; 4,500 kg

Walrus 3.3m; 1,200kg

Species	Average height/length (in m)	Average weight (in kg)

Now pick 3 of the animals, and in the box below, draw a visual representation to scale comparing the height, or length, of these animals. You may draw pictures of the animals, or use symbols to represent them.

1. Circle the animal that weighs the most per meter length:

Walrus	or	Asian Elephant
Polar Bear	or	West Indian Manatee
Wild Asian Water Buffalo	or	Eastern Lowland Gorilla
Orca	or	Humpback Whale

2. What observations can you make about the chart? _____

_____

_____

_____

_____

_____

_____

_____

_____

_____

_____

_____

_____

_____

Explore

In the Explore Cyberlab, you watched several videos about the way that scientists study animal behavior in the field. Use what you have learned from the videos, your notes, and from class discussions to help you complete the chart below. For each line, fill in one species you observed exhibiting the listed behavior, what that behavior looked like in this particular species, and 1 to 2 further Questions you have about the species and/or the specific behavior.

Behavior	Species' Name	Description of Behavior	Questions to ask about Behavior/Species
Swimming			
Porpoising			
Group Behaviors			
Feeding			
Nursing			
Breathing			

Explain

Vocabulary Review

Circle the correct answer for the Questions below.

1. What is the meaning of the word **foraging**?

   a. breeding

   b. observing underwater

   c. searching for food

   d. tracking

2. Which questions can researchers answer about marine mammals through the use of satellite tracking tags?

   a. how animals interact with other species

   b. where animals migrate

   c. how long animals stay underwater

   d. what foods the animal eats

3. Which of the following are challenges that field researchers may encounter when studying marine mammals?

   a. rough seas

   b. changing weather conditions

   c. observing multiple organisms

   d. all of the above

4. Explain at least **three** ways in which scientists study the behavior of marine animals.

_____

_____

_____

_____

_____

_____

_____

5. List four things that animal researchers record when studying animals in the field.

_____

_____

_____

_____

_____

The following paragraph is about the legislation that protects marine mammals, something you are studying. Fill in the paragraph below with the missing terms from the word bank below. Use Page 405 in your text to help you complete this activity.

Endangered Species Act	1972	Congress	threatened
permits	50 meters	protocols	coordinates

Studying animal behavior in the field can be very difficult. There are many _____

that scientists must follow. Many of the marine mammals they are trying to study are

_____, or endangered. In _____ the Marine Mammal

Protection Act was passed by _____. This law, along with the _____

_____ offers protection to marine mammals, but requires scientists to obtain across _____ to study the animals. Under these regulations,

humans are required to stay _____away from certain species of animals.

Although these regulations make it more challenging to conduct research, scientists realize

that the laws are in place for the safety of the animals.

In this Lesson you are learning about the features of mammals. Use Page 408 in your text to help you complete the bubble chart below. In each bubble, list one of the characteristics that mammals share.

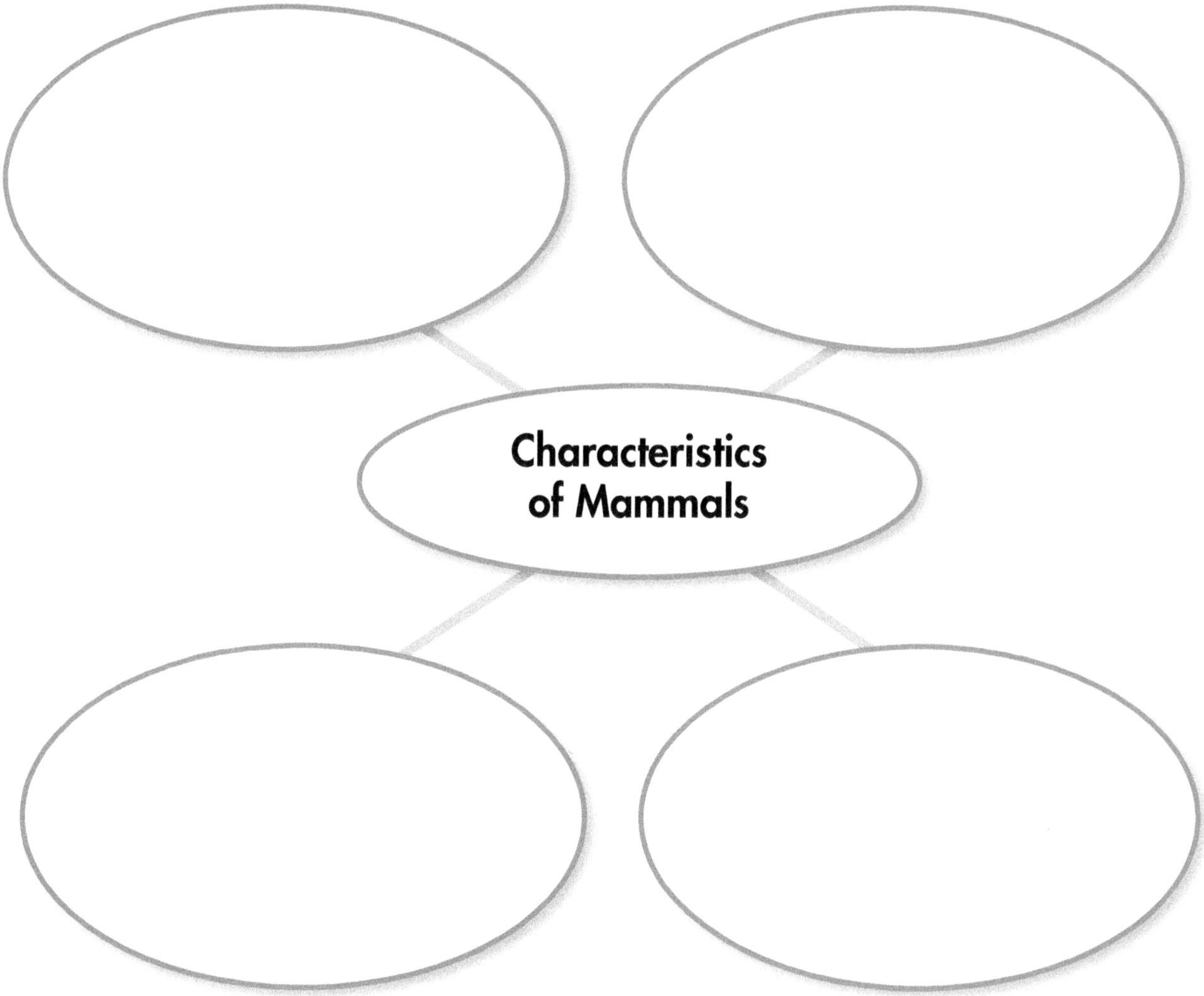

Characteristics of Mammals

1. List at least four different ecosystems where you can find marine mammals. _____

_____

_____

_____

_____

In Lesson 21 you are learning about various groups of marine mammals. One of these groups is the cetaceans. Below is a chart listing all the body parts of cetaceans. In each box, write the function of the body part listed. An example has been done for you.

Rostrum

Flukes

Blowhole

Body Parts of Cetaceans

Blubber

Teeth

In toothed whales, the teeth are used to eat fish, or squid, or to rip apart prey.

Baleen

Use Pages 408–409 in your textbook to help you fill in some of the three-way Venn diagram below, comparing three species of cetaceans. In each bubble, list one characteristic of the species and in the middle bubble, list one similarity they share.

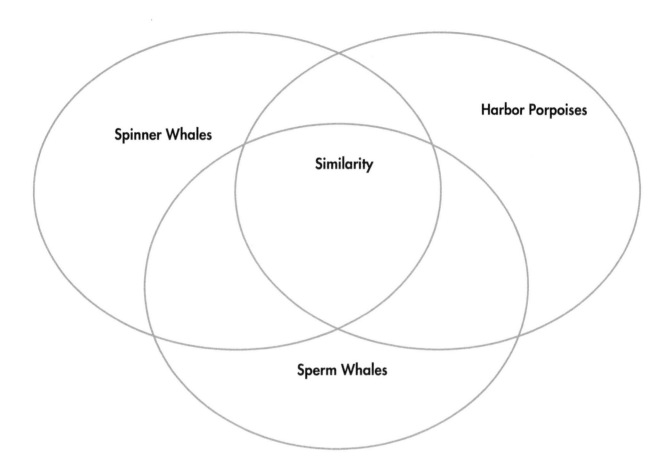

Use Pages 410–411 in your textbook to help you complete the chart below. Listed on this chart are the three types of pinnipeds. In the first three columns, list any information you know about the specific group of pinnipeds. In the last column, list characteristics that all pinnipeds share. Two examples have been done for you.

Pinnipeds

Eared Seals	True Seals	Walruses	Characteristics Common to all Pinnipeds
Includes seals with fur			Come on land to give birth and nurse their young

1. In which one of the following areas are manatees and dugongs **not** found?

   a. Eastern Africa

   b. The Caribbean

   c. The Arctic

   d. Australia

2. Sirenians are sometimes called what other name? _____

3. Describe at least **four** characteristics of sirenians. _____

_____

_____

_____

_____

_____

_____

_____

Read Page 411 in your text and search for the answers to the Polar Bear facts below.

1. Heat is trapped by a Polar Bear's _____.

2. Polar Bears spend most of their time on _____.

3. Their white fur helps them to _____.

4. Hair tubes on their body channel heat to their _____.

5. A Polar Bear's favorite prey is _____.

6. Polar Bears live throughout the _____.

7. There are this many Polar Bears worldwide _____.

8. Females can bear young when they are _____.

9. Polar Bears can live up to _____.

10. They build a den by digging into _____.

11. Cubs stay with the mother until they are _____.

12. Mothers teach their cubs how to survive in the _____

13. Polar Bears became endangered in _____

14. Areas along the Alaskan coast are _____

15. The areas on the mainland are used for _____

16. The areas on the sea ice are important for _____

Write true or false on the line next to each statement below. If the statement is false, explain why on the line below.

17. Sea otters are very closely related to marine mammals. _____

_____

18. Sea otters have water-resistant fur, instead of blubber. _____

_____

19. Sea otters use their sharp claws to break open shelled food. _____

_____

20. Sea otters have flipper-like hind limbs and no collarbone. _____

_____

21. Sea otters are found off the southern coasts of the United States and in warm ocean

waters. _____

_____

_____

In this Lesson you have learned that there are certain rules to abide by when observing animals in the wild. For every action a human may take, there are multiple negative effects that may occur, leading to unwanted outcomes.

Below are multiple cause and effect charts. In each chart, one cause is listed. Below the cause, there is space to list effects. Fill in the boxes with possible effects related to the cause. One example has been done for you. Use Pages 412–413 in your text to help you complete the activity.

Touching, handling, or riding animals may lead to

wiping scales off fish	

Feeding animals using food, or other decoys may lead to

Approaching, or chasing, wildlife in a boat, on foot, or in a car can cause animals to

Answer the following Questions.

1. Explain at least **three** negative outcomes that may occur when humans try to touch, or feed, animals in the wild. _____

   _____

   _____

   _____

2. What is a **stranding network**? _____

   _____

3. How do laws, such as the Endangered Species Act, protect marine mammals? _____

   _____

   _____

Elaborate

Vocabulary Review

Match the group behavior below with the statement that best describes that behavior. Use Pages 418–419 in your textbook to help you. Then, answer the Questions that follow.

1. _____ cooperative feeding

    a. whales swim in a circular pattern below prey and exhale bubbles which trap the fish in a cylinder of bubbles

2. _____ pectoral fin slapping

    b. a whale launches itself out of the water, landing on its back and creating a huge splash

3. _____ breaching

    c. a whale slaps its flukes on the water as a possible warning to other whales

4. _____ bubble netting

    d. whales work together to herd and stun prey

5. _____ spyhopping

    e. a whale rises vertically above the surface to see what is happening out of the water

6. _____ tail slapping

    f. a whale slaps its flippers on the water to communicate with other whales

7. How do scientists identify individual whales in the wild? _____

_____

_____

8. Why does knowing the names of individual whales help researchers in the field? _____

_____

_____

_____

_____

_____

_____

Evaluate

Lesson Review

When scientists study a particular species of animal, they record their findings, observations, data, and questions in a Field Journal.

Below is a sample Field Journal. You will pick a particular species you have learned about in Lesson 21. Use your text, notes, class discussions, videos, and cyberlabs to help you complete the necessary information below.

Species you studied: _____

Field Journal	
Average Weight/Height/Coloration:	**Structural Adaptations and their Functions:**
Habitats where the species can be found:	**Types of research conducted/used:**
Behaviors you observed in this species:	**Further questions you have about the species:**

Draw a sketch of the species you studied in the box below, labeling important characteristics/ features.

Lesson Summary

- There are a variety of mammals that either live in, or near the ocean, or depend on the ocean as a primary food source.

- Many of the mammals that live in the ocean are a much bigger size than their land counterparts.

- The density of the water supports this greater size.

- All mammals give birth to live young, nurse their young, are warm-blooded, and have hair.

- Many of these mammals participate in group behaviors such as swimming and feeding.

- These animals have special adaptations such as water-resistant fur and blubber to keep them warm in colder habitats.

- Scientists use satellite tracking tags and field research to study these animals.

- There are many laws and regulations in place to ensure the safety of these animals, as many are endangered, or threatened.

- Humans must be careful not to touch, or approach, animals in the wild, or they risk injuring themselves, or the animal.

22 Relationships in the Sea

BIGIDEAS

- Many kinds of marine species living in the same community interact with each other in special ways called symbiotic relationships.

- Reproduction, a relationship that occurs within a species, varies from species to species.

Engage

Activate Prior Knowledge

In this Lesson you will learn about relationships among species in which the organisms give and take from each other. In some relationships, two species interact in ways that benefit both of the species. In other relationships, one of the species benefits while the other is unaffected. In a third type of relationship, one of the species benefits and the other is harmed. Here is an example that may be familiar. At times, dogs may have fleas. A flea bites a dog and uses the dog's blood for food. The dog may develop skin or other health problems as a result. In this relationship, the flea benefits, and the dog is harmed.

Before reading and trying the activities in your textbook, use the chart below to preview and make predictions about relationships. Place a check mark in the box that correctly describes the relationship of the two species in each example. Then, name which organism or organisms benefit, which is unaffected, and which is harmed.

Example	One species benefits, the other is not affected	One species benefits, the other is harmed	Both species benefit
Aphids, tiny insects, are protected from predators by ants. Aphids make a sweet liquid that ants drink.			
A female mosquito bites a human to get blood to produce her eggs. The human develops an irritating, itchy bump.			
A seed head of a burdock plant attaches to the fur of a passing dog and falls off in a field, unnoticed by the dog. The seed head begins to grow in the field.			

Explore

Secondary Research on the Internet

On Pages 425–428 of your textbook, you are reading information and tips about how to conduct secondary research on the Internet. As you begin your research of symbiotic relationships, use these pages to help you gather information from several websites. Then, compare the websites to determine which ones will be useful.

1. Determine and write a good question or questions for you to research about symbiotic relationships.

   _____

   _____

2. When using a search engine to find information, you will enter specific search topic(s). What will your search topic(s) be?

   _____

   _____

3. After entering your search topic(s) in a search engine, do any "hits" look useful? Remember to use reliable sites, such as those that end in .gov, .edu, or .org. Try not to rely on sites with .com extensions. Record in the table on the next page any sites (by web address or URL) that you think may be useful. If you do not find useful sites at first, what other search topics will you try to refine your search?

   _____

   _____

4. For each site you list, scan the site and record other information about the site in the table. (An example is provided.) Afterwards, compare the entries in the table. Can you eliminate any sites? For example, suppose a site does not list a bibliography or any recent references, or has not been updated for many years. You might want to eliminate it from your list of resources.

Once you have found several reliable sites that will give you the information you need, you will be ready to write source cards and note cards as described on Pages 429–430 of your textbook.

URL/Web Address	Origin of Site (example: government, university, scientific encyclopedia, museum)	Bibliography or Other References (example: research books, scientific articles)	Recent Bibliography or Other References	Additional Links Provided?
http://web.uconn.edu/mcbstaff/graf/Sym.html	university	yes, texts and scientific research articles	yes	yes

Explain

Reading Strategy: MAIN IDEA AND DETAILS

Many facts and ideas are communicated in science. Arranging main ideas and details in a graphic organizer is a visual way to help you understand and remember how information fits together. One kind of graphic organizer is a concept map. The largest oval includes the broadest, most general topic. The smaller ovals show more specific content or details related to the general topic.

As you read about symbiotic relationships on Pages 432–433 of your textbook, complete the concept map below. Part of the map has been done for you. At the end of the Lesson, use your completed concept map as a study aid to review key concepts of the Lesson.

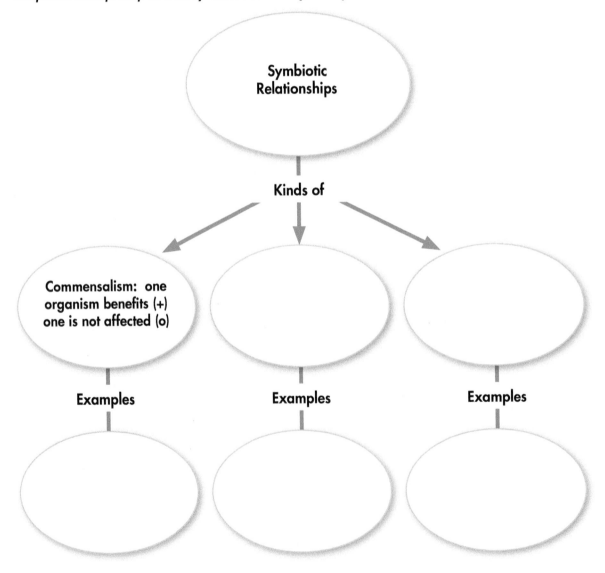

Vocabulary Review

After reading Pages 432–437 of your textbook, complete the sentences below with the correct term from the word bank.

host	coevolution	symbiotic	mutualism
interspecific	commensalism	intraspecific	parasitism

1. A crab which makes its home in a sponge while not affecting the sponge is an example of a relationship called _____.

2. In _____, each organism benefits from the relationship.

3. A relationship between two organisms of the same species is an _____ relationship.

4. The organism that is harmed in a symbiotic relationship is called the _____.

5. Over a long time, clownfish and sea anemone populations each developed genetic traits in response to each other. This process is called _____.

6. A relationship between two organisms of different species is an _____ relationship.

7. A worm living in the intestines of a fish is an example of _____.

8. Commensalism, mutualism, and parasitism are three kinds of _____ relationships.

Elaborate

Vocabulary Review

Complete the chart below as you read Pages 437–442 of your textbook. Write the definition of each vocabulary term in your own words. Then, write a note to yourself on how you can remember the meaning of each term. Use the chart to review key concepts after you have finished the Lesson.

Term	Definition	How I Will Remember
Asexual reproduction		
Sexual reproduction		
Budding		
Substrate		
Sessile		
Spawning		
Gametes		

Reading Strategy: TAKING NOTES

Taking notes while you read is an important tool that can help you remember key concepts. One way to take notes and keep new information organized is by using a data table. In a data table information is organized into rows and columns so that information can be viewed and compared easily.

On Pages 437–442 of your textbook, you will read about the unique ways in which some marine organisms reproduce as well as the benefits and disadvantages of each method of reproduction. As you read these pages, use the table below to help you outline key points.

Name of Species	Type of Reproduction	Special Notes about Method of Reproduction	Benefit(s)	Disadvantage(s)
Sponge	asexual	budding	little energy; no partner required	no genetic diversity since new sponges are identical to the parent
Coral	sexual			
Sea turtle				
Penguin				

Name of Species	Type of Reproduction	Special Notes about Method of Reproduction	Benefit(s)	Disadvantage(s)
Seahorse				
Shark species with external development				
Shark species with internal development				
Blue Whale				

Reading Strategy: COMPARE and CONTRAST

When you *compare* objects, events, or processes, you look for similarities. When you contrast objects, events, or processes, you look for differences. One way to show similarities and differences is to use a Venn diagram. In a Venn diagram, a circle or oval is used for each object, event, or process. Unique characteristics are listed in the outer part of each circle or oval. Shared characteristics are listed in the area where the circles or ovals overlap.

Use the information from the chart you just completed on Pages 253–254 of your workbook to help you compare and contrast the reproduction of two species of your choosing. List the similarities and differences in the Venn diagram below.

Species: _____   Species: _____

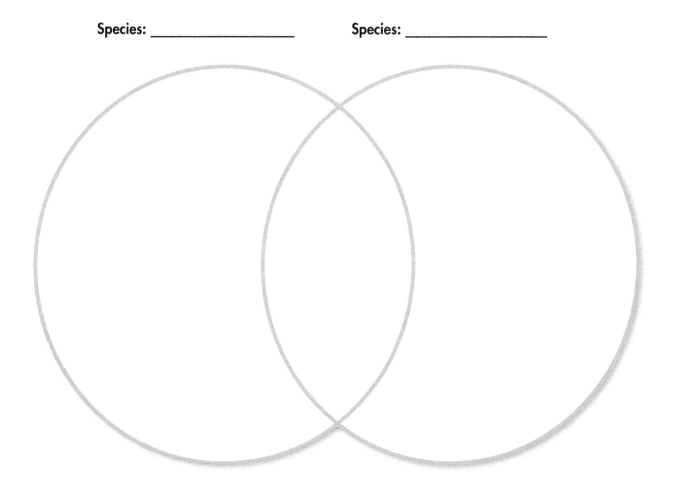

Evaluate

Lesson Summary

- In their work, scientists make use of a variety of secondary sources, such as scientific books and articles and the Internet.

- Secondary sources used in research must be valid, reliable, and cited.

- Symbiotic relationships, including commensalism, mutualism, and parasitism, exist between some species in order to ensure the survival of one or both species.

- In asexual reproduction, species reproduce without a partner, producing offspring that are not genetically diverse.

- There is no parental care among corals, and they must release large numbers of gametes to ensure that fertilization occurs.

- In sexual reproduction, fertilization happens when sperm and egg unite, usually during the union of two parents. Because offspring receive genetic material from two parents, offspring are genetically diverse.

- Many kinds of marine species, such as penguins, seahorses, whales, manatees, and some kinds of sharks, show various levels of parental involvement by one or both parents.

- The amount of energy invested in parental care among these marine species helps to ensure that their offspring live to adulthood in order to reproduce.

Organize Your Thoughts

On Page 431 of your textbook, you are asked to compare and contrast mutualism, parasitism, and commensalism. A data table can be used to help organize your ideas.

Complete the table below. Then, use the information in the table to compare mutualism, parasitism, and commensalism.

Characteristic	Mutualism	Parasitism	Commensalism
Number of species in relationship			
Number that benefit			
Number that are harmed			
Number that are unaffected			

23 The Ocean's Waves

BIG IDEAS

- Ocean waves develop as a result of wind, and like all waves, are a form of energy transfer.

- Characteristics of waves, such as wavelength, period, frequency, and speed, can be measured and calculated.

- Waves impact organisms living on or near the coast.

Engage

In this Lesson, you will learn about waves, how they form, and how they impact marine organisms. Use the chart below to record what you already know about these ideas. After you complete the Lesson, use the chart to record new information you learned.

Before reading and trying the activities in your textbook, think about the Questions below. Record what you know about each topic in the What I Know column of the chart.

Question	What I Know	What I Learned
How do ocean waves form?		
How do waves affect landforms?		
How do waves affect marine and coastal organisms?		
How are waves important to people?		

Explore

Review What You Learned

After trying the activity on Page 446 of your textbook, answer the Questions below to review what you learned.

1. Describe what happened when you and your classmates created the two different types of waves. _____

   _____

   _____

2. In what direction did energy flow in each wave? _____

   _____

   _____

3. Did the energy (or movement of the wave) flow in the same direction as the students moved? _____

   _____

   _____

4. Did these results surprise you? Why or why not? _____

   _____

   _____

5. Do you think ocean waves are more similar to the first wave you and your classmates created, or the second? Why? _____

   _____

   _____

Name Class Date

Explain

Vocabulary Review

Complete the chart below as you read Pages 447–455 of your textbook. Write the definition of each vocabulary term in your own words. Then, write a note to yourself on how you can remember the meaning of each term. Use the chart to review key concepts after you have finished the Lesson.

Term	Definition	How I Will Remember
Medium		
Wave		
Crest		
Trough		
Transverse wave		
Orbital wave		

Term	Definition	How I Will Remember
Longitudinal wave		
Frequency		
Wave period		
Scatter plot		
Fetch		
Wave train		
Rogue wave		

Reading Strategy: COMPARE and CONTRAST

Pages 447–449 of your textbook describe three types of waves—transverse waves, longitudinal waves, and orbital waves. Comparing and contrasting the characteristics of these waves can help you better understand each type of wave. Remember when we compare, we tell how things are alike. When we contrast, we tell how things differ.

Use the Venn diagram below to explore similarities and differences of transverse, longitudinal, and orbital waves.

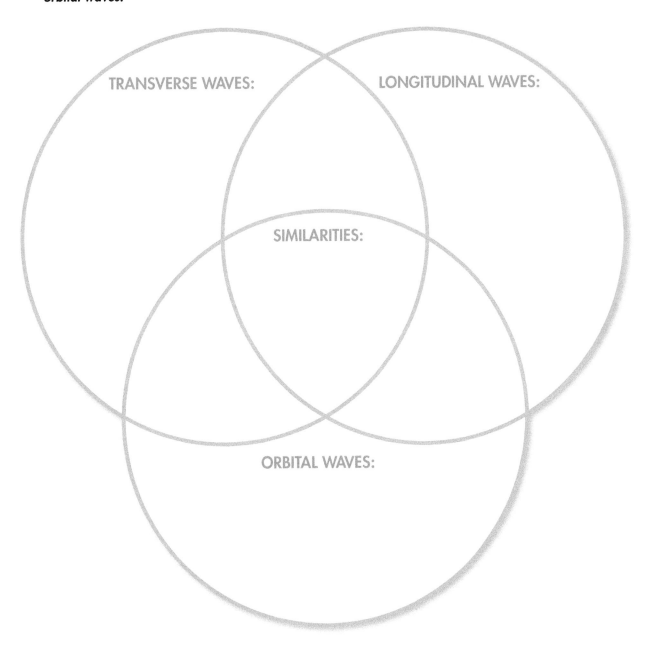

TRANSVERSE WAVES:

LONGITUDINAL WAVES:

SIMILARITIES:

ORBITAL WAVES:

Math Mini-Lesson

Pages 454–455 of your textbook show you how to calculate the speed and frequency of a wave. Scientists often make calculations when they measure things, analyze data, and explain events or observations.

Use the formulas and the examples below to practice calculating speed and frequency.

The formula used to calculate the speed of a wave is:

$$\text{speed} = \frac{\text{wavelength}}{\text{period}}$$

Here's an example. Suppose a buoy in the Atlantic Ocean near the Florida coast is reporting a dominant wave period of 4 seconds and a wavelength of 40 meters. What is the speed of the wave?

Based on the formula we need to know the wavelength and period of a wave to calculate its speed. Read the example again and write the wavelength and period in the spaces below.

wavelength = _____

period = _____

Now you can insert these numbers into the equation and calculate the wave's speed.

speed = _____ = _____

Now that you know the speed of the wave you can also calculate the frequency of the wave.

The formula used to calculate the frequency of a wave is:

$$\text{frequency} = \frac{\text{speed}}{\text{wavelength}}$$

Calculate the frequency of the wave described above. Insert the speed you calculated and the wavelength from the original problem into the formula.

Frequency = _____ = _____

These same steps can be used to calculate the speed of the tsunami wave on Page 455 of your textbook.

Review What You Learned

After reading Pages 447–453 of your textbook, answer the Questions below to review what you learned.

1. What kind of wave is an ocean wave? How does this help explain why things bob up and down on the surface of the water? _____

   _____

   _____

2. Can you feel waves on the seafloor? Why or why not? _____

   _____

   _____

3. How are the period and frequency of a wave related? _____

   _____

   _____

4. Describe in your own words how an ocean wave forms. _____

   _____

   _____

5. Why can storms generate larger waves in the Pacific Ocean than the Atlantic Ocean?

   _____

   _____

   _____

Organize Information

Pages 457–460 of your textbook describe the unique communities that inhabit sand dunes in Florida. Sand dune communities include three main zones. As you read about each zone, list the plants that live there as well as how the zone is affected by waves in the table below.

Sand Dune Zone	Plants	Impact of Waves
Pioneer Zone		
Scrub Zone		
Forest Zone		

Elaborate

Visual Literacy: Reading Maps

You know that scientists use maps as a visual tool for showing information. On Page 461 of your textbook, a map is used to show wave power density around coastlines. Both the map in your textbook and the map on the next page in this workbook show how something is distributed around a geographic region. Maps such as these are called distribution maps. They use color to compare numbers or degrees of things. Knowing how to read these maps is an important skill.

The map on the next page shows how many people are living in different areas of the world. The countries that are dark blue have higher populations (more people living in them) than the countries that are light blue. As the intensity of the blue increases, the population also increases.

GLOBAL POPULATION DENSITY

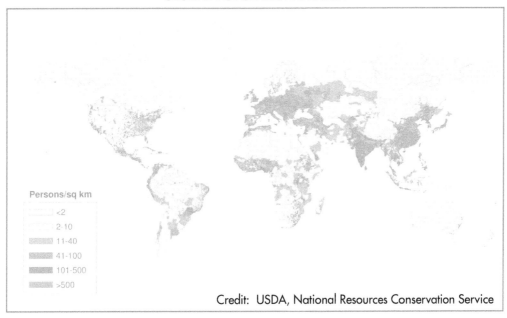

Persons/sq km

    <2
    2-10
    11-40
    41-100
    101-500
    >500

Credit: USDA, National Resources Conservation Service

Use the map above to answer the following Questions and practice your map reading skills.

1. According to the map above, does eastern South America or Australia have a higher

    population density? _____

2. According to the map, which region of North America has the lowest population density:

    Florida, Canada, or central Texas? _____

    _____

Answer the following Questions using the map on Page 461 of your textbook.

3. What do the purple dots on the map indicate? What do the blue dots indicate?

    _____

    _____

4. What color dots are there near the coast closest to where you live? Based on this
    information would your coast be a good location to harness the energy of waves?

    _____

    _____

    _____

Evaluate

Lesson Summary

- Waves are disturbances that travel through a medium. Waves differ from one another in the direction that the medium flows as compared to the direction of the wave.

- Waves can be characterized by wave height, wavelength, period, speed, and frequency.

- Wave height is influenced by many things including wind speed, wind duration, water depth, fetch, and nearby land masses.

- Plants living in sand dune communities are impacted by waves and salt water.

- Waves can be a source of both recreation and power for humans. However, rogue waves and tsunami waves can cause serious destruction.

- Wave energy is a renewable resource that can be harnessed and used to power our homes and businesses.

- The power of waves varies by location.

- There are positive and negative impacts of wave power plants.

Lesson Review

Turn back to Page 257 of this workbook and record information you gained from the Lesson in the What I Learned column of the chart. Then, use this information as well as your notes and other workbook pages to write a summary of the Lesson in your own words.

_____

_____

_____

_____

_____

_____

_____

24 A Time For Tides

BIGIDEAS

- The various motions of the ocean, namely tides, currents, and waves, are the result of a number of different influences.

- Tides directly affect the behavior of many marine organisms.

Engage

Activate Prior Knowledge

Below is an anticipation guide. It includes statements related to what you will read in this Lesson. Some of the statements are accurate, while others are not. Completing an anticipation guide before you read can help you recall information you know about a topic and become prepared for reading.

Before reading the Lesson, review each statement below and record whether you agree or disagree with the statement. Use what you have learned in the previous Lessons to help you make your decisions and explain your reasoning using your own words. When you have finished the Lesson, you will return to the anticipation guide to review your responses and compare them with what you have learned.

Statement	Agree/ Disagree	Explanation
Water level along a shoreline remains the same both day and night.		
Waves are usually higher during and just after a storm.		
Spring tides happen only in the spring.		

Statements	Agree/ Disagree	Explanation
Because the Sun is more massive than the Moon, it has a greater influence on the tides.		
Waves are caused by winds.		
Ocean currents are caused by waves.		
The action of waves causes many sea stars to perish.		
Many shoreline organisms had to develop adaptations to live in this type of habitat.		

Explore

Math Mini Lesson

The activity on Pages 470–474 of your textbook asks you to calculate the mean tidal range for several locations for March 2010. Below we will calculate the mean tidal range for Port Canaveral. Mean is another word for average.

Study the formula below. Then, answer the Questions that follow to review finding means.

To find the mean of a set of values, use this formula:

$$\text{Mean} = \frac{\text{sum of the values}}{\text{the total number of values}}$$

1. Finding the mean tidal range for Port Canaveral, Florida for the month of March requires several steps. First you must find the mean of the high tides. Describe the process for doing this first step.

    _____

    _____

2. What is the total number of values you will divide by?

    _____

    _____

    Hint: Look carefully at the table on Page 471 of your textbook. Notice that not every day has two high tides.

3. What must you find next? Describe the process. _____

    _____

4. What is the total number of values you will divide by? _____

    _____

5. Describe what you must do for the last step (finding the Port Canaveral mean tidal range).

    _____

Now that you have identified the steps for determining mean tidal range, complete step 6 on Page 474 of your textbook.

Name _____ Class _____ Date _____

Explain

Vocabulary Review

Complete the chart below as you read Pages 475–479 of your textbook. Write the definition of each vocabulary term in your own words. Then, write a note to yourself on how you can remember the meaning of each term. Use the chart to review key concepts after you have finished the Lesson.

Vocabulary Term	Definition	How I Remember
Gravitational force/ Gravity		
Spring tides		
Neap tides		
Surf zone		
Longshore currents		
Rip currents		

Name _____   Class _____   Date _____

Reading Strategy: COMPARE and CONTRAST

Pages 479–480 of your textbook compare and contrast waves, tides, and currents. Remember, to compare means to describe similarities. To contrast, means to describe differences. Organizing similarities and differences in a Venn diagram is a visual way to help you understand and remember key concepts.

As you read about waves, tides, and currents, use your own words to list the similarities and differences between them in the Venn diagram below. When you have completed the diagram, use it as a study aid to review key concepts from the Lesson.

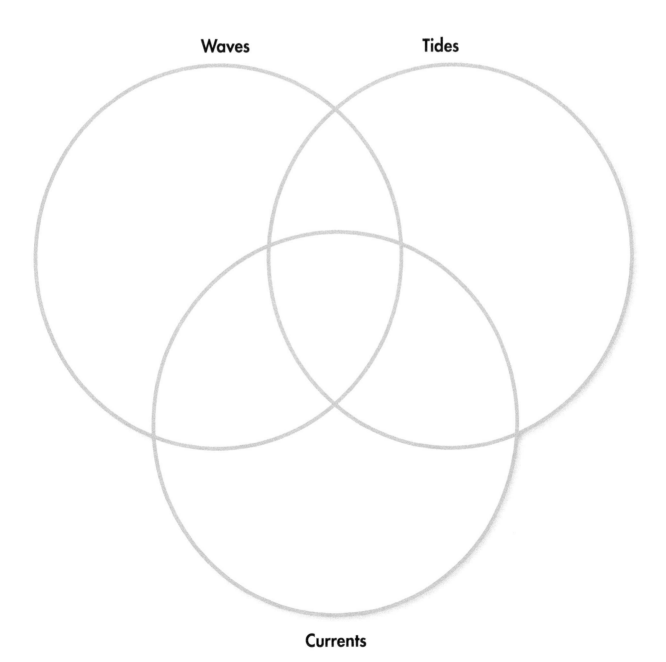

Waves

Tides

Currents

Elaborate

Reading Strategy: TAKING NOTES

The Elaborate section of your textbook describes coastal ecosystems and ways in which tides affect the organisms living there. Recall that taking notes as you read is an important tool that can help you remember key concepts. One way to take notes and keep new information organized is by using a concept map such as the one below.

As you read about several kinds of coastal ecosystems on Pages 481–484 of your textbook, use the concept map to record key ideas.

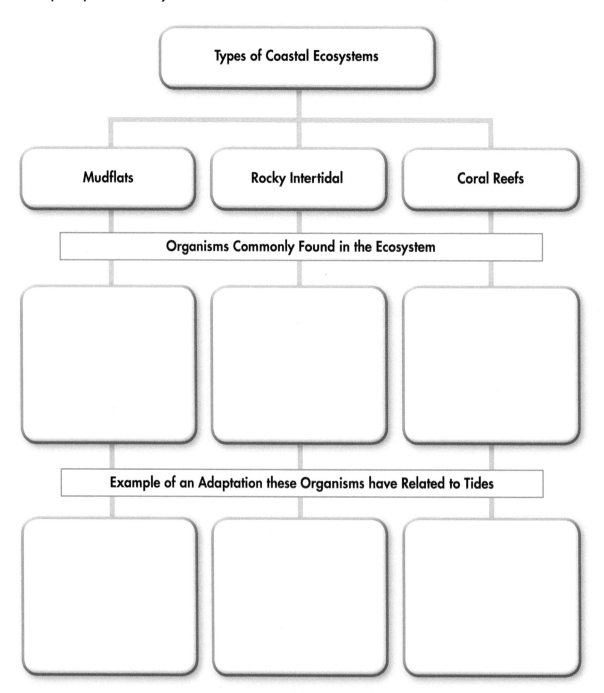

On Pages 482–483, you will read about some organisms that live in a narrow coastal area between the high tide and low tide. This area, the intertidal zone, is made up of four zones. As you read about each of these zones, identify them and record their characteristics in the graphic organizer below. Then, use the information from the organizer to answer the Questions that follow.

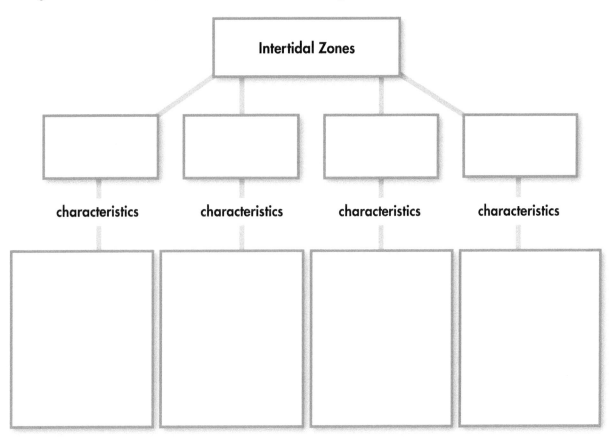

1. Which zone is exposed to air and direct sunlight most? Least? _____

   _____

2. Why couldn't a sea star live in the splash zone? _____

   _____

3. In which zone or zones are you likely to find mussels? Explain why. _____

   _____

   _____

Evaluate

Lesson Summary

- The gravitational pull of the Moon and the Sun cause bulges in Earth's atmosphere and water.

- The gravitational effects of the Moon and Sun are responsible for Earth's tides, the rise and fall of the ocean's surface, several times each day.

- The highest high tides, spring tides, occur about twice each month when the Earth, Sun, and Moon are in a straight line (at full moon and new moon phases).

- The tides with the least difference between high tide and low tide, neap tides, occur about twice each month when the Earth, Sun, and Moon form a perpendicular angle to one another (about seven days after each spring tide).

- Waves, tides, and currents all contain energy of motion.

- Waves are the result of winds transferring energy from the atmosphere to the ocean.

- Large, persistent surface currents are caused by prevailing winds.

- Tidal movements influence behaviors and adaptations of many marine organisms, including grunions, sea turtles, corals, Christmas Tree Worms, and brittle stars. Tides impact how and when organisms reproduce, as well as how they find food, and how and where they move to.

- Intertidal ecosystems, such as the rocky intertidal and mudflats, have four major zones. These include the splash zone, the high-intertidal zone, the mid-intertidal zone, and the low-intertidal zone.

- Each part of the intertidal zone has a different exposure to air, wind, sunlight, and water. This affects the number and species of marine organisms that are able to live in each zone.

Now that you have completed the Lesson, read each statement in the anticipation guide again. Decide if you still agree or disagree with the statement. Then, decide if you agree with your original explanation, or if you would like to change it. In the Explanation column, write a reason why the statement is true, or change your explanation so that it is correct.

Lesson Review

Use what you have learned in this Lesson and the word bank to help you fill in the blanks in the statements below.

1. The patterns of rise and fall of the ocean's surface are called _____.

2. _____ are often found in coastal ecosystems and in estuaries, where rivers deposit large amounts of sediment.

3. About twice a month, _____ occur when the Sun, Moon, and Earth form a perpendicular angle to one another.

4. Most coastlines on Earth experience a _____ tide pattern, with two high and two low tides a day.

5. Although the gravitational pull of the _____ on the Earth is greater, it has less of an effect in Earth's tidal changes because it is further from the Earth than the _____.

6. _____ and _____ determine the strength of the gravitational attraction between objects.

7. _____ is the vertical distance between the high and low tide lines.

8. Some locations experience only one high and one low tide a day, which is called a _____ tide cycle.

9. Rocky intertidal ecosystems usually have the most _____, or rocky areas

   filled with water.

10. _____ occur when an area experiences the highest high tides and their

    lowest low tides.

BONUS: What is a tidal bore? _____

_____

_____

_____

_____

_____

_____

_____

25 Animal Needs and Animal Tracking

BIGIDEAS

- Dissolved oxygen in the ocean comes from the atmosphere and the process of photosynthesis.

- Marine animals obtain oxygen and nutrients with the help of upwelling and ocean eddies.

Engage

Activate Prior Knowledge

In this Lesson, you will learn about oxygen in the ocean and how certain ocean areas become rich in oxygen and nutrients. Before reading and trying the activities in your textbook, record if you agree or disagree with each statement in the anticipation guide below. Remember that some of the statements in an anticipation guide are accurate, while others are not.

Topic	Agree/ Disagree	Explanation
Phytoplankton provide more than half of the oxygen in Earth's atmosphere.		
Humans could not exist without phytoplankton.		
Many organisms use upwelling areas in the ocean as feeding grounds.		

Name _____ Class _____ Date _____

Topic	Agree/ Disagree	Explanation
Cold-core eddies are not typically an area where marine animals feed.		
Warm water expands more than cold water because the molecules release heat.		
The height of the sea surface is affected by wind.		

Explore

Practice Process Skills: ANALYZE DATA

The Cyberlab on Pages 490–491 of your textbook asks you to analyze data of dissolved oxygen and water temperature. Remember that when you analyze data you study information that has been collected and look for patterns or relationships in the information. Often, scientists create graphs to help them analyze data from research or experiments. One type of graph they use often is a line graph. Line graphs help show trends in data—for example, how one variable is affected by the other as it increases or decreases. If enough data are collected, you can make predictions about data not yet collected.

Before trying the activity in your textbook, look at the graph on the next page and answer the Questions that follow to practice analyzing data with graphs.

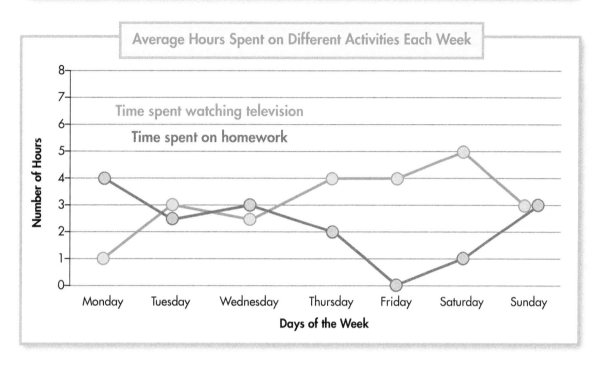

Average Hours Spent on Different Activities Each Week

Time spent watching television

Time spent on homework

Number of Hours

Days of the Week

1. What information is shown along the x-axis?

_____

Hint:
The x-axis is the horizontal axis.
The y-axis is the vertical axis.

2. What information is shown along the y-axis?

_____

3. What is represented by the blue line? The gray line?

_____

_____

4. On which day does this student watch the most television? The least?

_____

5. Do the number of hours spent on homework increase, decrease, or stay about the same throughout the week?

_____

6. Is there a relationship between the number of hours spent watching television and the number of hours spent on homework?

_____

_____

Explain

Vocabulary Review

Complete the chart below as you read Pages 491–494 of your textbook. Write the definitions of each vocabulary term in your own words. Then, write a note to yourself on how you can remember the meaning of each term. Use the chart to review key concepts after you have finished the Lesson.

Term	Definition	How I Will Remember
Upwelling		
Limiting factor		
Bloom		
Relaxation		

Visual Literacy: Reading Images

The Explain section of your textbook shows several satellite images for you to analyze and interpret. Remember from previous Lessons that satellites collect sea surface temperature (SST) data and read chlorophyll concentrations. The data they collect are sent to computers that color code the data and create satellite images. The images are like data maps—they show information about geographical areas. Knowing how to read these images is an important skill.

Use the images on Page 491 of your textbook to answer the following Questions.

1. What do the color bars below each image show?

   _____

   _____

2. What does dark green represent on the SST image?

   _____

3. What does dark orange represent on the chlorophyll concentration image?

   _____

4. Where is the concentration of chlorophyll highest in the chlorophyll image?

   _____

5. What is the temperature where chlorophyll concentrations are highest?

   _____

6. Find the areas on the SST image where temperatures are about 27 °C. Find the same areas on the chlorophyll concentration image. Is chlorophyll concentration high or low in these areas?

   _____

7. What is the relationship between chlorophyll concentration and phytoplankton population?

   _____

   _____

Elaborate

In the Elaborate section of your text, you are learning about eddies. Use the Venn diagram below to compare and contrast cold-core and warm-core eddies. Make sure to include at least 3 differences and 3 similarities.

Cold-Core Eddies

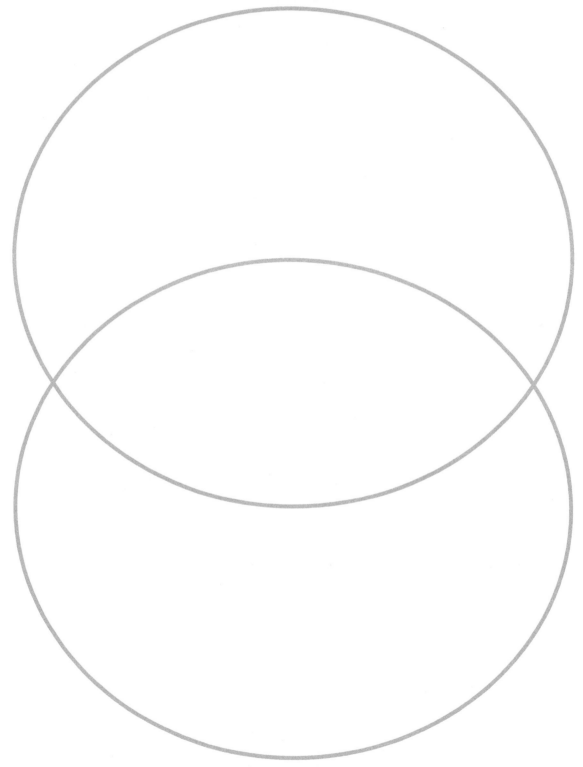

Warm-Core Eddies

Practice Process Skills: INFER

Scientists use the process of scientific inquiry to investigate and learn about our world. Many times they make an educated guess to explain something they observe. When scientists use their prior knowledge and combine it with factual observations to explain certain phenomena or events, they are making an inference. Here's an example from everyday life. When you hear a siren, you might infer that it's coming from a fire engine without seeing one. You might infer a smell is coming from cookies baking in the oven without actually looking in the oven. Making inferences is an important part of the scientific process, and it is a skill you will use as you analyze data and answer Questions in this Lesson.

Read the scenarios below and write an inference to explain each scenario in the space provided. Be sure to support your inference with details.

1. On a summer vacation at the beach, you started a rock collection. All of the rocks you collected while walking along the shore were rounded and smooth. The diameter of these rocks was no larger than that of a quarter. After a severe coastal storm hammered the coastline for two days, you discover a large, round boulder on the beach. How did the boulder get on the beach?

    _____

    _____

    _____

    _____

2. You have an aquarium filled with goldfish in your living room. You notice one day that there are not as many goldfish in the aquarium as the day before. You count fifteen goldfish in the tank before you leave for school. When you return home, you only have twelve. The next morning there are ten goldfish. Water droplets are on the floor near the aquarium, and fish food is sprinkled on the table surface. What is happening to the goldfish?

    _____

    _____

    _____

    _____

Evaluate

Lesson Summary

- Most organisms require oxygen in order to obtain energy from food.

- Cold water holds more dissolved oxygen than warm water.

- Upwelling results when cold, nutrient-rich water rises to the surface. Many organisms use these nutrient-rich areas as feeding grounds.

- Wind and bathymetry affect upwelling. Areas off the coast with steep continental slopes tend to generate much upwelling when the wind conditions are right.

- Marine animals that obtain their oxygen from the water have developed specialized gills for extracting the oxygen from the water.

- Eddies are swirling rings of ocean water. Cold-core eddies are nutrient rich and are highly productive areas for marine organisms. Warm-core eddies can have an impact on weather through evaporation and heat transfer.

Lesson Review

Answer the Questions below to review key concepts of the Lesson.

1. Describe the process of respiration in organisms.

   _____

   _____

   _____

   _____

2. Compare the amount of salts dissolved in the ocean to the amount of water in the ocean.

   _____

   _____

   _____

   _____

3. What is the relationship between water temperature and dissolved oxygen?

_____

_____

_____

_____

_____

_____

4. What is upwelling and how is it important to marine organisms?

_____

_____

_____

_____

_____

_____

5. Describe two types of eddies. What is the relationship between eddies and currents?

_____

_____

_____

_____

_____

_____

6. What is sea surface height and what can scientists use it to calculate?

_____

_____

_____

_____

_____

_____

Return to the anticipation guide that you completed in the beginning of the Lesson. Review each statement again. Decide if you still agree with your original answers, or if you would like to change your responses. In the Explanation column, write a one-sentence reason proving why the statement is true, or changing the statement so that it is correct.

26 Student Expert Research

- Conducting secondary research and analyzing data are important steps in scientific inquiry.

- You can apply what you learn through research to track and analyze marine animal movement.

Engage

Activate Prior Knowledge

In this Lesson, you will conduct research to become Experts in one of four areas of Marine Science. Before you begin the Lesson, complete the chart below to review what you already know about each of the environmental parameters listed.

Description of the Environmental Parameter	How Do Satellite Images Help Us Learn About This Parameter?	How Does This Parameter Affect Marine Organisms?
Bathymetry		
Phytoplankton		
Sea Surface Conditions		

Explore

Visual Literacy: Reading Satellite Imagery

The activity on Pages 505–508 of your textbook asks you to use and interpret satellite imagery. Recall that satellite imagery provides information about Earth's surface such as SSTs and chlorophyll concentration.

Before beginning the activity in your textbook, answer the following Questions to review your understanding of satellite imagery.

1. What does the color bar associated with a satellite image show? _____

    _____

    _____

2. Look at Figure 26.2 in your textbook. In your own words, how would you describe the

    SSTs around the coast of Florida? _____

    _____

    _____

3. What is shown in Figure 26.6 of your textbook? _____

    _____

    _____

4. Which colors are used to indicate features on land? Which colors indicate features below

    the water's surface? _____

    _____

    _____

5. What does 0 meters on the color bar represent? _____

_____

_____

6. In Figure 26.8, what is shown on the image's color bar? _____

_____

_____

7. In Figure 26.8, what does black represent on the color bar? White? Deep blue? _____

_____

_____

8. What is shown in Figure 26.9? What does this image help us locate and track? _____

_____

_____

9. In Figure 26.9, what do the dark blue colors represent? The orange and red colors?

_____

_____

_____

10. In which month are chlorophyll concentrations generally highest according to the images

in Figure 26.9.? _____

_____

Explain

Team 1: Species Expert Research

If you are a member of Team 1, you will conduct secondary research to answer questions about marine species. Recall from Lesson 22 that there are many research sources you can use. Sources include books, interviews with experts, scientific encyclopedias, articles from magazines, and Internet websites. Each kind of source has its advantages and disadvantages. Remember that all sources used should be reliable and current.

Use the table below to help you organize your research. Enter sources you find that may help you answer your Questions. Then, go back and decide individually or as a group which sources you want to use and which you want to eliminate. Adjust the table to meet your needs.

Source	Title and Pages or URL	Authors	Copyright or Last Update	Affiliation (university, museum, etc.)
Encyclopedia				
Books				
Websites				
Articles				

Team 2: Bathymetry Expert Research

If you are a member of Team 2, you will research and graph features of the seafloor in four marine sanctuaries. Then you will prepare a short report of your findings.

Use the table below to help organize your data and prepare your report.

Name of Sanctuary	Location of Sanctuary (near what state/in which ocean?)	Seafloor Depth	Description of Bathymetry (types and number of features)

Team 3: Phytoplankton Expert Research

If you are a member of Team 3, you will interpret chlorophyll imagery to understand changes in phytoplankton populations better. You will need to include details about chlorophyll concentrations for different parts of the ocean as well as for different times of the year.

As you view the chlorophyll images, use the following tables to record your observations. Then, use the information in the tables to answer the Questions in your textbook.

Description of Phytoplankton in the Atlantic Ocean and Gulf of Mexico (East Coast)

2006	2007
Jan.	Jan.
Apr.	Apr.
Aug.	Aug.

Description of Phytoplankton in the Pacific Ocean (West Coast)

2006	2007
Jan.	Jan.
Apr.	Apr.
Aug.	Aug.

Team 4: Sea Surface Expert Research

If you are a member of Team 4, you will view SST imagery for a number of National Marine Sanctuaries. Then you will write a short report to address several Questions on Pages 516–517 of your textbook.

As you view the SST imagery, record information in the appropriate rows and columns of the table below. Then, use the information in the table to help you write your report.

Name of Marine Sanctuary	Latitude	Mean January 2007 SST	Mean April 2007 SST	Mean August 2007 SST

Elaborate

Organize Your Thoughts

On Page 519 of your textbook, you are asked to answer Questions that you and your classmates had about the ocean and animal tracking. Use the table below to record your team's Questions, answers, and a list of sources that you used to answer each Question.

(Name of Expert Team) _____

Question	Answer	Data or Sources Used

Evaluate

The Elaborate section of your textbook asks you to make a 5–7 minute presentation to your class about your research findings.

As a team, plan your presentation, making decisions about the following Questions:

☐ Which questions and answers should be presented?

☐ What should the order of the questions and answers be?

☐ What data and images should be used to support and clarify the research?

☐ How will the work be broken up?

Practice your presentation several times with your team. Refine it as you go. The more you practice, the more comfortable and confident you will feel delivering the information.

Here are some Questions to help guide you as you practice the presentation:

☐ Have we stayed within the 5–7 minute time period?

☐ Do we speak clearly and with confidence?

☐ For each question we present, do we stick to the question?

☐ For each question we present, do we give enough information to answer the question?

☐ For each question and answer we present, is there a clear organization with a beginning, middle, and end?

☐ Are facts and conclusions supported by reliable sources and not opinions?

☐ Do graphs, tables, and other images help to explain and clarify ideas?

27 Student Expert Analysis

BIGIDEAS

- Sea surface data help scientists track animals and analyze their movements.

- Satellites enable scientists to track animals in real-time and gather environmental data that can be analyzed and compared.

- The results of individual studies can help the entire scientific community learn more about species and their range and movement.

Engage

Activate Prior Knowledge

In this Lesson you will follow the animal you have been assigned. As you follow the satellite tracking maps you will learn what it means to be a Marine Species Expert.

Think about what you learned about research in the previous Lesson. Use your own words to answer each Question below.

1. What is a Student Expert Team? _____

    _____

    _____

2. Why is it helpful to study animals in the wild? _____

    _____

    _____

3. What is bathymetry? Why do we track chlorophyll concentrations? What kind of sea

    surface data do we measure? _____

    _____

    _____

4. How is the work of Student Expert Teams similar to the work done by scientists? _____

_____

_____

5. In one to three sentences, state your hypothesis for how your animal will move over the

course of the study. _____

_____

You have been assigned an animal to track. It is likely that you know something about this animal from your studies thus far. What are some of this animal's features or habits? Think about where the animal lives. What kind of marine ecosystem does it call home? What does it eat?

Use the left column of the chart below to record what you already know about the animal. Then, think about what you hope to learn during your student expert study. Write those details in the center column. After the study, return to this chart and summarize what you learned about your animal in the last column of the chart.

What I Know	What I Want to Know	What I Learned

Explore

Practice Process Skills: INFER

Throughout this Lesson you will analyze data from images, maps, tables, and graphs to understand animal movements. You will also make inferences about why animals move or behave in a certain way. Remember that when you make an inference, you use prior knowledge and experience to explain an observation. Making inferences is an important part of the inquiry process. Inferring helps scientists integrate data and events in order to form meaningful ideas that can be tested or researched further.

Before doing the activity, review how to make inferences with the following activities. For Questions 1–4, classify the statements as observations or inferences.

> When deciding if something is an observation or inference, ask yourself: Does the statement explain what happens (observation) or why something happens (inference.)

1. The Humpback Whale made a noise underwater to call for its young. _____

2. The seals lie on a sunny rock off of the coast. _____

3. The temperature of ocean water decreases with depth. _____

4. The debris from a volcano caused organisms to move to new locations. _____

For Questions 5–10, make an inference to explain why each event happens.

5. A snake approached a lizard. The lizard spit a thick black substance in the direction of

    the snake. _____

    _____

    _____

    _____

6. A non-poisonous butterfly species has evolved over time to have the same coloring and

   patterns as a poisonous moth. _____

   _____

   _____

   _____

7. Phytoplankton populations are highest near coastlines. _____

   _____

   _____

   _____

8. The area of sea ice near the Arctic Circle is shrinking. Polar Bears are moving farther

   North. _____

   _____

   _____

   _____

9. Shortly after a storm a variety of marine organisms were spotted along the coast in areas

   where they are not usually found. _____

   _____

   _____

   _____

10. After lionfish were introduced on the coast, native species began to disappear. _____

   _____

   _____

Math Mini-Lesson

During your Student Expert Analysis, you will be asked to make calculations that will help you analyze your data and better understand your animal. Read the text and answer the Questions below to review some of the calculations you may be asked to make.

Elapsed Time. Elapsed time describes the time between two events. To calculate elapsed time, you can count up from the starting time to the ending time.

Practice calculating elapsed time in hours with Questions 1–3. Remember, the length of a complete day is 24 hours. The length of time between a morning (a.m.) hour and its afternoon or evening (p.m.) hour is 12 hours (there are 12 hours between 8 a.m. and 8 p.m.).

1. Leo tracked a whale swimming between 11:30 and 2:15. For how long did he track the whale's movement? _____

2. Monica tracked a sea turtle between 3:15 p.m. on Tuesday and 9:30 a.m. on Wednesday. For how long did she track the sea turtle? _____

3. A shark began swimming from one island to another at 10:20 a.m. and arrived at 11:10 a.m. How long did it take the shark to get from island to island? _____

Practice calculating elapsed time in days, weeks, and months with Questions 4–6. Use a calendar to help you.

4. A Loggerhead Sea Turtle is tracked from March 15th to May 30th. How many weeks were spent tracking the animal? _____

5. Jorge tracked a sea lion from November 1st to December 17th. For how many days did he track the animal? How many weeks? _____

6. Tang spent 42 days tracking a Humpback Whale. She started on January 11th. What day did she finish her tracking? _____

Calculating Speed. While studying your animal, you may want to find out how fast it travels from place to place. You can calculate the average speed of an object using the following equation:

$$\text{speed} = \frac{\text{distance}}{\text{time}}$$

Use the equation above to find the average speed of the following animals.

1. A turtle travels 2 kilometers in ½ hour. What is the turtle's average speed?

   _____

2. It takes a whale 3 hours to travel 160 kilometers. What is the whale's speed?

   _____

3. In a 24 hour period, a shark travels one thousand kilometers. What is the average speed

   that the shark traveled during this time? _____

   _____

Finding the Mean. When studying your animal, you may find a set of data, such as temperature or depth that changes over time. It is helpful to find the *mean*, or average, value of the data set. You can find the mean of a data set using this equation:

$$\text{Mean} = \frac{\text{sum of values in data set}}{\text{number of values in data set}}$$

Find the mean of the following data sets.

1. 23 °C, 35 °C, 27 °C, 36 °C, 30 °C _____

2. 35 ppm, 32 ppm, 33 ppm, 35 ppm _____

3. 1,000 meters, 1,233 meters, 650 meters, 938 meters, 1,052 meters, 897 meters

   _____

Explain

Practice Process Skills: COMMUNICATE

As you begin your Student Expert Analysis, you will record observations, inferences, and new questions you have about your animal in a journal. That is, you will communicate information about your animal. When you communicate, you share information and ideas with others. By sharing information, we work collaboratively and help to build a body of scientific knowledge that can be accessed by all.

Read the journal entry below, then answer the Questions that follow to review your communication skills.

The Loggerhead Sea Turtle

Observations:

The movements of a Loggerhead Sea Turtle named Lily were observed between March 2 and April 6 of this year. The team that took the observations was the Sea Surface Expert Team. The animal's location, as well as the general conditions of its sea surface environment only, were observed and analyzed. The environmental conditions observed included temperature and surface current data. The chart below lists the SST observations of the water over a month where Lily was tracked.

Date	Water Temperature
3/2	68 °C
3/8	65 °C
3/16	74 °C
3/27	66 °C
4/6	65 °C

The following additional observations were made about Lily by the Sea Surface Expert Team:

- Lily traveled quickly through warmer areas of water and lingered in warmer places.

- Lily traveled 1,520 kilometers (944 miles) between the first and last day of tracking.

Explanations:

Lily prefers warm water environments in the time period for various reasons which include her need to survive and thrive.

Answer the following Questions about Lily and the journal entry.

1. How many days was Lily studied during the observation period?

   _____

   _____

2. Which was easier to analyze and see quickly—the water temperature data shown in a table or the list of water depths in the text? How might you communicate observations and data in your journal entries?

   _____

   _____

   _____

   _____

3. What data would help support the analysis that Lily "lingered in warm water" and "traveled quickly through cold water"? How could this observation be made stronger?

   _____

   _____

   _____

   _____

4. What questions might you ask Bathymetry, Phytoplankton, or Marine Species Experts?

   _____

   _____

   _____

   _____

   _____

Elaborate

Review What You Learned (after tracking the animal for a period of weeks or months)

During the study, the class' teams gathered information about the animals that were assigned. Collectively, the groups learned about the water depths over where it traveled. Teams learned the water temperature of the areas and something about the surface ocean currents. Teams learned about the food with phytoplankton maps. There was other information learned. The class might wish to know more to get a full understanding of the animal and the challenges it faces in its environment.

Complete the table below with collaboration from other team members to help you understand what the study means.

Were the results about your animal what you expected when you started the study? Why or why not?	
What fact did you find most surprising about your animal and your observation of it?	
What are the biggest challenges your animal faces in its habitat?	
Does human activity affect your animal and its environment? How?	
What do you think your animal's chances for survival are? Why do you think this?	
What else might you want to learn about your animal?	
How might someone else's data about the same kind of animal help you to better understand your own data?	

Evaluate

Lesson Review

1. How do student research projects help the scientific community as a whole? _____

   _____

   _____

2. Why must scientists record data as they work? _____

   _____

   _____

3. What are some benefits of studying animals with satellite systems? _____

   _____

   _____

4. What are some drawbacks of studying animals with satellite systems? _____

   _____

   _____

5. Would the results of an animal study be exactly the same if it were repeated? Why or why

   not? _____

   _____

   _____

6. Why is it important for scientific data to be as accurate as possible? _____

   _____

   _____

28 Which Way to the Sea?

BIGIDEAS

- Every body of water, large and small, has a watershed. Smaller watersheds drain into larger watersheds that drain into the ocean.

- Various chemical and physical characteristics of a body of water influence its quality.

- The quality of ocean water is directly related to the quality of the freshwater bodies that drain into it.

Engage

Activate Prior Knowledge

As you begin this Lesson, you will view an e-Tools video about the water cycle. After viewing the video, complete the sequence of events diagram below to identify the major steps of the water cycle. Then, answer the Questions that follow to review what you already know about this cycle.

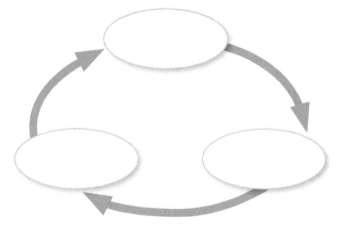

Although each step of the water cycle is occurring at all times, the steps of any one drop of water follow a general sequence.

1. Over where do clouds bring precipitation? _____

_____

_____

2. What are evaporation and condensation? _____

_____

3. What are the sources of water, mentioned in the video, that feed the water cycle? _____

_____

_____

Explore

Visual Literacy: Reading Maps

The activities on Pages 545–549 of your textbook ask you to interpret maps. Remember that maps are pictures used to show information about a place. When you look at a map, be sure to notice such things as the use of shading, symbols, lines, and numbers, as well as the information provided in keys, labels, and captions.

Use the maps on Pages 545–547 of your textbook to answer the following Questions.

1. What is highlighted in Figure 28.4 on Page 545 of your textbook? How is this area

    highlighted? _____

    _____

2. According to Figure 28.4, which smaller watersheds make up the Mississippi River

    watershed? _____

    _____

3. What does Figure 28.5 show? _____

    _____

4. According to Figure 28.7, which states are included in the Missouri watershed? _____

    _____

    _____

    _____

5. What does Figure 28.8 show? _____

    _____

    _____

On Pages 547–549 of your textbook, you are reading about and working with **topographic maps**. They have contour lines to show the shape and elevation of the land.

Use the text to help you answer the Questions below and then complete the contour map activity.

1. What types of landforms do topographic maps show? _____

_____

_____

2. What are contour lines? _____

_____

_____

3. What does the distance between contour lines indicate? _____

_____

_____

_____

_____

The top of this drawing is a contour map showing the hills that are illustrated at the bottom. On this map, the vertical distance between each contour line is 10 feet.

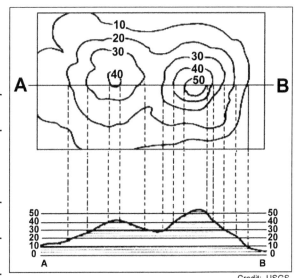

Credit: USGS

1. Which is higher, hill A or hill B? _____

2. Which is steeper, hill A or hill B? _____

3. How many feet of elevation are there

   between contour lines? _____

4. How high is hill A? _____

   How high is hill B? _____

5. Is the slope of the terrain greater on hill A

   or hill B? _____

Explain

Vocabulary Review

As you read Pages 550–553 of your textbook, define each vocabulary term in your own words. Then, write a note to yourself on how you can remember the meaning of each term.

Term	Definition	How I Will Remember
Wetland		
Floodplain		
Headwaters		
Groundwater		
Aquifer		
Springs		
Delta		

Review What You Learned

After reading about freshwater systems on Pages 550–553 of your textbook, answer the following Questions to review what you learned.

1. What are some freshwater systems and what do they all share in common? _____

   _____

   _____

2. What is the function of aquifers and why are they so important? _____

   _____

   _____

3. Compare the way in which water flows at higher elevations to the way it flows at lower

   elevations. _____

   _____

   _____

4. When water flows, it weathers and erodes materials. What are some materials that water

   carries in a river system? _____

   _____

   _____

5. Explain why floodplains are good for farming. _____

   _____

   _____

   _____

Vocabulary Review

Use Pages 554–558 to help you match each term with the definition that best describes it.

1. ____ Riparian vegetation

    a. A measure of the amount of oxygen in water

2. ____ Turbidity

    b. A measure of the average kinetic energy of molecules

3. ____ Parameter

    c. A process in which a water body becomes depleted of oxygen as a result of excessive algae growth

4. ____ Secchi disk/turbidity tube

    d. A measure of how easily light can penetrate through water

5. ____ pH

    e. The type of plants along the banks of a freshwater body

6. ____ Temperature

    f. Nutrients in bodies of water needed by organisms to build proteins and DNA

7. ____ Nitrogen/phosphorus

    g. Tools used to measure water clarity

8. ____ Eutrophication

    h. A measure of how acidic or basic a substance is

9. ____ Dissolved oxygen

    i. A measurable characteristic

Reading Strategy: CAUSE and EFFECT

On Pages 554–558 of your textbook, you are reading how various chemical and physical factors affect the quality of fresh water and the organisms that live in it. Identifying cause-and-effect relationships such as these can help you understand events. Remember, a cause is the reason something happens. The effect is what happens as a result. In science, many actions cause other actions to happen.

As you read Pages 554–558, look for cause-and-effect relationships. Using your own words, describe several of these relationships in the chart below.

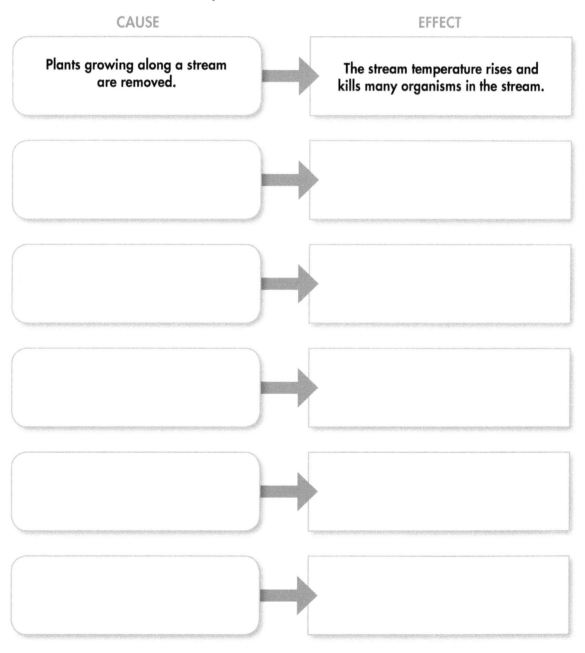

CAUSE

EFFECT

Plants growing along a stream are removed.

The stream temperature rises and kills many organisms in the stream.

Elaborate

Practice Process Skills: RECORD DATA

The lab on Pages 559–561 of your textbook asks you to make detailed field notes for your watershed survey. Field notes are an important part of collecting data. It is helpful to decide ahead of time the kinds of things you want to observe and record about the sampling area. This information can be organized as headings in a table. When you get to the sampling area, you can use the table to record your observations.

The table below lists some suggestions of observations you might want to make for the physical assessment. You may add, delete, or change any information in the table. After the table has been revised, use it to record notes about the local watershed.

Shape of the body of water	
Riparian vegetation (location, amount, types)	
Bank conditions (steepness, evidence of erosion)	
Evidence of debris (large rocks, overhanging trees, etc.)	
Human disturbances (pavement, boat ramps, docks, removal, or addition of vegetation, etc.)	
Other notable aspects	

Evaluate

Lesson Summary

- Because smaller watersheds are contained in larger watersheds that drain into the ocean, the quality and health of local watersheds affect the quality and health of the ocean.

- Topographic maps may be used to identify local watersheds.

- Earth's fresh water is stored in lakes, ponds, rivers, streams, wetlands, ice, snow, and underground aquifers.

- Fresh water is a resource that is important to all organisms.

- The geology and topography of the land determine the path of a river or stream.

- As water flows, it picks up, transports, and deposits things, such as salts, minerals, and sediments.

- Scientists sample bodies of water, surveying chemical and physical parameters to determine water quality.

- Special tests and tools are used to measure chemical parameters such as nitrogen and phosphorus, turbidity, temperature, pH, and dissolved oxygen.

- Scientists also survey the physical parameters of a body of water to determine water quality. Some physical parameters include the size and depth of the water body, the water's velocity, the physical condition of the banks, the amount and type of vegetation along the banks, the size and location of sediment, and observations of human activity within the watershed area.

Lesson Review

Write a summary of what you learned in this Lesson. Start by recording the main ideas of the Lesson in the graphic organizer below. Then, use the main ideas to structure your summary.

Main Idea	Main Idea	Main Idea	Main Idea

SUMMARY

29 Nonpoint Source Pollution

BIGIDEAS

- Human activities on land have an impact on the ocean's ecosystems.

- Nutrients added to bodies of water affect the growth of algae and phytoplankton.

Engage

Activate Prior Knowledge

In this Lesson you will build on your understanding of phytoplankton, photosynthesis, and chlorophyll imagery from previous Lessons. Before reading and trying the activities in your textbook, answer the following Questions to review what you already know about these topics.

1. What is photosynthesis? _____

   _____

2. What are some examples of producers? _____

   _____

3. What are phytoplankton? _____

   _____

4. What materials are required for photosynthesis? _____

   _____

5. What is chlorophyll? _____

   _____

6. What do satellite images of chlorophyll concentrations show us? _____

   _____

Explore

Practice Process Skills: REVIEW

The lab on Pages 567–568 of your textbook asks you to perform an experiment over a two-week period of time. You will need to design your own experiment and set up your own procedures. The question you are trying to answer is: How do light or nutrients affect phytoplankton growth? To answer this question, you'll need to use many of your science skills. Review them by reading the text and completing the activities that follow.

Define Variables. In a controlled experiment, you must test only one factor, or variable, at a time. Remember, the independent variable is what you change in an experiment. It's the variable you want to test to find out its effect. For this experiment, your independent variable is either the amount of nutrients or the amount of sunlight the phytoplankton receive—not both. The dependent variable is what you are measuring in the experiment. The control variables are the factors that are kept the same throughout the experiment.

Fill out the following chart to define your variables and help organize and set up your experiment.

Independent Variable	Dependent Variable	Control Variables

1. What can you do to test how light affects phytoplankton growth? Hint: Think about where you might place each bottle. _____

   _____

2. What can you do to test how nutrients affect phytoplankton growth? Hint: Think about what you should add to one or both bottles. _____

   _____

3. What factors should you keep the same in each experimental bottle? Why should these

variables be controlled? _____

_____

_____

Make Observations. We make observations every day. Remember, making observations requires the use of our five senses to gather information. We can make observations by taking measurements (quantitative), or by describing something in words (qualitative). Often times, scientists make both quantitative and qualitative observations during an experiment.

Classify each statement below as qualitative or quantitative. Then, answer the Questions that follow.

4. The plant grew 5 cm in height. _____

5. The water changed from clear to cloudy. _____

6. There is 10 mL of water in the beaker. _____

7. We added 10 grams of salt to the water. _____

8. After adding the unknown powder to Solution B, the solution bubbled. _____

9. What kinds of observations do you think you might make in this lab? _____

_____

10. Why do you think it is important to make your observations of each bottle at about the

same time? _____

_____

Collect and Record Data. Making observations is a way of collecting data. In order to analyze and draw conclusions from data, it is important to record your data in a clear and organized way. Using data tables to record data is a simple and effective way of doing this.

Before setting up your data table for the lab, there are a few Questions you need to ask yourself so that you create space for all your data.

11. How long will the experiment last? When will you make observations? _____

_____

12. From how many experimental bottles will I be collecting data? Is it important to keep

observations of each bottle separate? _____

_____

13. How am I collecting my data? Am I measuring something (quantitative) or am I

describing changes I see (qualitative)? _____

_____

14. Will I need space for additional comments or notes to keep track things that I may

change, or add to the experimental bottles? _____

_____

Communicate Results. After all your data have been collected, you will need to communicate your findings to your classmates. You can use words, pictures, graphs, tables, or charts to describe your experiment, results, and conclusions.

15. How might you explain your findings to your classmates? _____

_____

_____

_____

Review What You Learned

After reading Pages 568–571 in your textbook and watching the e-Tools video, answer the Questions below to review what you learned.

1. Explain the following terms in your own words:

   Dead zone—_____

   _____

   Hypoxic—_____

   _____

2. Describe four factors that result in the Gulf of Mexico's Dead Zone.

   1. _____

      _____

   2. _____

      _____

   3. _____

      _____

   4. _____

      _____

3. What factors eventually break up the Gulf of Mexico's Dead Zone? _____

   _____

   _____

Explain

You have been reading in Lesson 29 about the different types of marine pollution and the causes of each. Below is a **Cause/Effect chart**. Listed on one side of the chart are causes of different types of marine pollution. On the other side of the chart are the negative effects caused by pollution entering the water through varying means.

Use your knowledge of the subject and Pages 568–576 in your text to help you fill in the blank boxes in the chart. The first row has been done for you as an example.

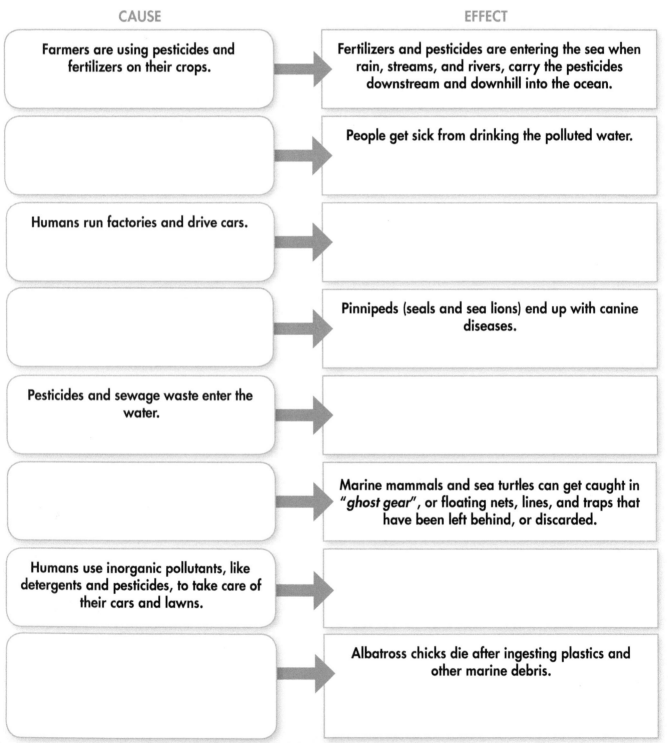

CAUSE	EFFECT
Farmers are using pesticides and fertilizers on their crops.	Fertilizers and pesticides are entering the sea when rain, streams, and rivers, carry the pesticides downstream and downhill into the ocean.
	People get sick from drinking the polluted water.
Humans run factories and drive cars.	
	Pinnipeds (seals and sea lions) end up with canine diseases.
Pesticides and sewage waste enter the water.	
	Marine mammals and sea turtles can get caught in *"ghost gear"*, or floating nets, lines, and traps that have been left behind, or discarded.
Humans use inorganic pollutants, like detergents and pesticides, to take care of their cars and lawns.	
	Albatross chicks die after ingesting plastics and other marine debris.

Reading Strategy: SEQUENCE OF EVENTS

Pages 568–571 of your textbook describe the process of eutrophication and the sequence of events that lead to this problem. Knowing the sequence of events in which something happens can help you understand a process.

After reading Pages 568–571 in your textbook, read the statements below and number them in order to correctly sequence the steps that lead up to eutrophication.

_____ Phytoplankton begin to die and sink to the bottom of the sea.

_____ Producers, such as algae living attached to rocks on the seafloor, may die, as will the animals that feed on these organisms.

_____ A "blanket" is created on the surface of the water, through which light cannot penetrate.

_____ Excess nutrients are present, causing phytoplankton to reproduce at a much faster rate.

_____ Hypoxic conditions exist, causing the death of fish, invertebrates, and other organisms.

_____ Bacteria begin to take over the aquatic ecosystem.

_____ The phytoplankton continue reproducing until they can no longer meet their own needs and use up their resources.

_____ Marine plants and small animals may die.

_____ The sudden increase in the amount of phytoplankton in the seawater causes a bloom which upsets the balance in the marine ecosystem.

_____ Decomposers remove the oxygen from the water to break down the tissues of these dead organisms.

1. What two inorganic elements are important nutrients for phytoplankton? _____

_____

2. What human sources can result in an excess of nutrients? _____

_____

_____

Vocabulary Review

After reading Pages 571–576 of your textbook, complete the vocabulary activities below to review key concepts. For Questions 1–4, match each term with the correct definition or example.

1. _____ Natural pollution

   a. Solids, liquids, gases, or even living things that do not belong in an environment

2. _____ Marine debris

   b. Result from human activities; human centered.

3. _____ Pollutant

   c. Pollution caused by volcanic eruption

4. _____ Anthropogenic

   d. Any solid material that persists in the ocean, such as a plastic bottle cap

For Questions 5–8, draw a line to match each type of pollution or pollutant to its appropriate example.

5. Nonpoint source pollution   Metals and detergents

6. Inorganic pollutants   Sewage, pesticides, oil, and gas

7. Organic pollutants   Oil spills and smoke from smokestacks

8. Point source pollution   Fertilizers or pesticides carried by water many miles to the sea

Fill in the paragraph below with the missing terms from the word bank below. Use Pages 574–575 in your text to help you.

| biodegradable | reduce | recycle | plastic nodules | reuse |

One of the biggest contributors to marine pollution is plastics. Many types of plastics are not _____ and do not completely break down, or decompose. Some plastics do break down partially into _____ , or tiny particles that get mixed with sand and plankton floating on the ocean surface. Plastics, both large and small, can be hazardous to marine organisms and shorebirds. By making more environmentally conscious choices, such as using metal water bottles or cloth lunchbags, we can _____ the amount of trash we make. Like glass, metal, and paper, we can also _____ some plastics and turn them into new products. Alternatively, instead of throwing out plastic containers we can _____ them for other things. Then we can be a part of the pollution solution instead of the problem.

Elaborate

In the Lab in the Elaborate section of your text, you are asked to complete a survey. A survey is a method of gathering information, or collecting data from a sample of individuals, or locations. Surveys can involve people, or can be to inventory items. Surveys are a helpful way to find out about many topics and to amass facts about the topics, in order to either study it further, or to address a particular issue. In this Lesson, you are conducting a Marine Debris Survey. During the survey you are gathering trash around your school to determine the most common items that are found, and addressing what problems these items might cause for marine ecosystems.

Below is a sample survey conducted on a mile-long stretch of beach. For this survey, debris was separated into two categories. Land-based debris included items such as syringes, metal cans, balloons, six pack rings, straws, plastic bags, and plastic bottles. Ocean-based debris included oil/ gas containers, light bulbs/tubes from boats, nets, traps, poles, fishing line, rope, and floats/buoys.

Use the data, your knowledge of the topic and your experience with surveys to help you answer the Questions that follow.

Beach Debris Survey

Type of Item	Number of Items Found
Ocean Based Items:	
Oil/Gas containers	13
Nets	15
Traps	20
Poles	11
Fishing Line	26
Pieces of Rope	33
Floats/Buoys	18
Light Bulbs/Tubes	22
Land-Based Items:	
Syringes	16
Metal Cans	42
Balloons	28
Six Pack rings	39
Straws	18
Plastic Bags	47
Plastic Bottles	56
TOTAL:	404

1. Make three observations about the data found in the table above. _____

   _____

   _____

   _____

   _____

2. What item counted had the highest total? Lowest? Why do you think this might be the

   case? _____

   _____

   _____

   _____

3. Was there a higher total of land-based pollutants, or ocean-based pollutants? Why do

   you think this is? _____

   _____

   _____

4. What items on this survey were different from the survey you conducted at your school?

   Why would you be more likely to find these items on a beach, than at a school? _____

   _____

   _____

   _____

   _____

5. Choose three items from the table above and describe how you think these items ended

   up as pollutants on the beach. _____

   _____

   _____

   _____

6. Pick two items and describe how they might be harmful to marine species. _____

_____

_____

_____

7. Name two steps you could take to eliminate some of the debris found during this survey.

_____

_____

Conduct Your Own Survey

Pick 6 types of debris from the above table. Conduct a brief survey of your classmates to determine which type of debris they think is most harmful. Record your answers in the table below.

Type of Debris	Number of Students who think it is the most harmful type

Write two observations based on your quick survey and the information in your data table.

_____

_____

_____

Evaluate

Lesson Summary

- Many human activities on land, such as farming and fertilizing lawns, have an impact on ocean ecosystems.

- Satellite imagery that measures chlorophyll concentrations helps us locate algal blooms.

- Algal blooms can occur as a result of natural or human-made causes and can be dangerous to humans and other organisms.

- The Mississippi River flows into the Gulf of Mexico, depositing fresh water that flows from 31 states. This water contains many nutrients from farming and other activities and can lead to dangerous algal blooms.

- The process of eutrophication begins with the addition of excessive nutrients into a body of water. The nutrients create ideal conditions for phytoplankton to grow and reproduce rapidly. Once their needs can no longer be met, the phytoplankton die. Decomposers (bacteria) break down the dead organisms and consume the water's available oxygen. This results in hypoxia.

- Hypoxia is a condition in which the concentration of dissolved oxygen in water is very low. Hypoxic conditions can lead to the death of marine organisms.

- A dead zone is a phenomenon in coastal waters that results from hypoxic conditions and their effect on marine organisms.

- The Gulf of Mexico Dead Zone is linked to a seasonal change, usually occurring in late spring and early summer. The Dead Zone remains present until late August and early September (hurricane season) when strong storms mix the upper level Gulf waters with the lower level waters.

Lesson Review

A **problem-solution chart** is an organizer that lists problems in one column and ways to fix those problems in the other column. It allows you to easily organize information about a particular topic. In your text, you are reading about the problem of marine debris. As a result of marine pollution, many species of fish and marine organisms are becoming sick, dying, or losing their habitats. Our ocean resource is being negatively affected. In your text, several suggestions have been given as solutions to these problems.

Use the Explain section of your text, your class discussions and your own ideas to fill in the boxes below. The first row has been completed as an example.

Problem	Solution
Poorly maintained waste systems aboard boats leads to the release of sewage, oil, and gas leaks.	Boat owners should make sure their waste system and pump out stations are checked each year to ensure they are working properly.
Fertilizers and detergents enter the water when humans wash their cars, or take care of their lawns.	
Organic pollutants, like pet waste, enter the water and introduce disease and parasites.	
	Fishing boats and even boaters out for pleasure must make sure to be responsible for their gear. They must dispose of unusable gear responsibly.
Plastic nodules, from partially degraded plastics, get mixed in with phytoplankton and sand and cause disease and death in marine animals.	
	NOAA has established a marine debris program to educate the public about this issue. We can follow their guidelines and help educate others.

1. What types of pollution have you seen near your home that could potentially end up as marine debris? What problems might this type of pollution cause? What is one solution you could suggest that would address this problem?

_____

_____

_____

_____

_____

_____

_____

_____

_____

_____

_____

_____

30 Point Source Pollution

BIGIDEAS

- Pollution can be caused by natural sources or by human activities.

- Marine pollution can have devastating effects on animal populations, habitats, and ecosystems.

- Oil spills can have long-lasting and catastrophic effects on animals, humans, and ecosystems.

- Because marine pollution is harmful to our ocean, we need to develop solutions to address the issue in order to save its resources for future generations.

Engage

Activate Prior Knowledge

Below is an anticipation guide. It includes statements related to what you are reading in this Lesson. Some of the statements are accurate, while others are not. Completing an anticipation guide before you read can help you recall information you know about a topic. It can help you to become prepared for reading about the topic. When you have finished the Lesson, you will return to the anticipation guide to review your responses and compare them with what you have learned.

Before reading and trying the activities in your textbook, review each statement in the anticipation guide and record whether you agree or disagree with the statement.

Statement	Agree/ Disagree	Explanation
All point source pollution occurs directly in the ocean.		
Marine pollution has, at times, necessitated the closing of certain bodies of water.		

Statement	Agree/ Disagree	Explanation
Intentional dumping is illegal and therefore no longer a problem, as it was in the past.		
The ocean is so large that marine pollution isn't really a problem.		
The source of marine pollution is often difficult to trace.		
Most oil in the ocean is from point source pollution, such as oil spills.		
Leaky cars and faulty gas pumps are examples of nonpoint source oil pollution.		
There is usually one correct way to best clean up an oil spill.		
Marine pollution affects only the specific location where it occurs.		
Marine pollution is harmful to marine organisms.		
The three Rs (reducing, reusing, and recycling waste) are ways to help prevent or minimize pollution.		

Explore

Review What You Learned

In the Explore section of your textbook, you are asked to follow the Engineering Design Process to solve a problem. After completing the lab, use the table below to review the process and what you learned.

Steps in the Engineering Design Process	What It Means (definition in your own words)	What You Did in Your Oil Spill Experiment
1. Identify the Need or the Problem	Figure out what question you are trying to answer. What is the problem that you need to address?	Talk to your group members and discuss that you will be trying to solve the problem of cleaning up a coastline oil spill and how to determine the best way of doing this.
2. Research the Need or Problem		
3. Develop Possible Solutions		

Steps in the Engineering Design Process	What It Means (definition in your own words)	What You Did in Your Oil Spill Experiment
4. Select the Best Possible Solutions		
5. Construct a Prototype		
6. Test and Evaluate the Solution(s)		
7. Communicate the Solution		
8. Redesign		

Use the table, the text, and your experiences during the lab to answer the following Questions.

1. What do you think was the most important step of the Engineering Design Process and why?

   _____

   _____

   _____

   _____

2. What was the best source your group used to research the problem? Why?

   _____

   _____

   _____

   _____

3. If you could change one part of the process, or add or delete a step, what would you change and why?

   _____

   _____

   _____

   _____

4. Think of and explain another situation where using the Engineering Design Process might be helpful. How could you use some of these steps to help you solve your problem and come up with a working solution?

   _____

   _____

   _____

   _____

Explain

Vocabulary Review

As you read Pages 588–597 of your textbook, define each vocabulary term in your own words. Then, write a note to yourself on how you can remember the meaning of each term.

Term	Definition	How I Will Remember
Wastewater Treatment Plants		
Sewers		
Fossil Fuels		
Offshore Drilling		
Anoxic		

Term	Definition	How I Will Remember
Deepwater Drilling		
Plumes		
Tar Balls		

Use Pages 588–597 of your text to complete the activities below.

Put a number next to each of the steps below to show the correct order in which water is treated at a wastewater treatment plant.

_____ The water is treated and disinfected.

_____ Wastewater from toilets and sinks is collected in sewers.

_____ Clean water is released into local bodies of water.

_____ Particles are removed.

_____ Bacteria are used to consume organic matter, such as feces.

_____ Sewers carry human waste to a treatment plant.

1. List at least three examples of point source pollution in the ocean.

   _____

   _____

   _____

   _____

   _____

   _____

2. What is the Clean Water Act and what effect did it have on marine pollution?

   _____

   _____

   _____

   _____

   _____

   _____

3. What is the main difference between the General Electric (GE) incident in upstate New York in the 1970s and the incident at the aluminum plant in Hungary in 2010? How were these events similar?

   _____

   _____

   _____

   _____

Fill in the boxes below to explain how fossil fuels are formed.

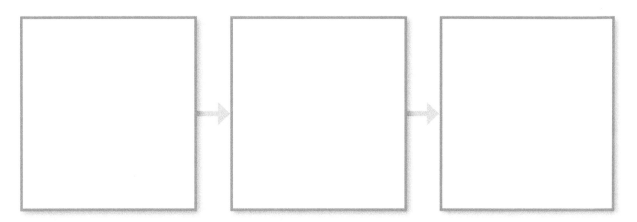

Reflect on Your Reading

Pages 591–594 of your textbook explain the processes of offshore and deepwater drilling. Some people think that we should continue these methods of removing oil and natural gas from the seafloor, while other people believe that these processes are detrimental.

Use a Pros and Cons scale to record the benefits (Pros) and problems (Cons) related to relying on the ocean and drilling in the seafloor.

Pros	Cons

In the Explain section of your textbook, you are learning about how oil spills can affect different marine animals.

In the bubbles below, list at least three ways in which oil spills impact that particular species. Use Pages 599–603 of your textbook to help you complete the activity. An example has been done for you.

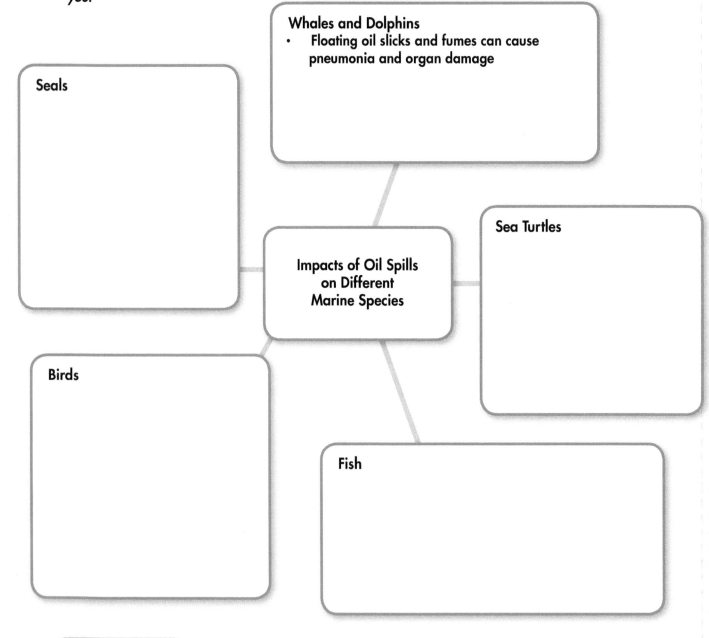

Seals

Whales and Dolphins
- Floating oil slicks and fumes can cause pneumonia and organ damage

Sea Turtles

Impacts of Oil Spills on Different Marine Species

Birds

Fish

Elaborate

In the Elaborate section of your textbook, you are asked to research and debate the idea of using dispersants as the major method for oil spill cleanup. You use a Dispersants Note Sheet to help you keep track of your ideas and facts about this method. On the next page is a similar type of organizer. This time you are picking a different cleanup method and answering the Questions in each box in relation to the method of your choosing.

Use your textbook, the labs you have completed, the Marine Science: The Dynamic Ocean *website, and your class discussions to help you complete the activity.*

Cleanup method you are choosing _____

What effect does your cleanup method have on the oil?

What effect does your method have on the physical environment? The biological system? Present any past data from other oil spills to support your statements.

What will happen to the oil if this method is not used? Is the effect of this method more or less harmful to the environment than oil that is dispersed?

Final comments/proposal

Evaluate

Lesson Summary

- As the world's population increases, humans are putting more strain on Earth's resources.

- Pollution is harmful to the land, the air, and freshwater and marine environments.

- Fossil fuels found on the seafloor, formed over millions of years, are extracted through drilling processes.

- Drilling for oil has both positive and negative effects and is a hotly debated topic.

- Although intentional dumping is now illegal in many areas, accidents causing pollution still happen.

- Contamination events like oil spills and sewage leaks can be dramatic and devastating to marine ecosystems.

- There are many ways to clean up oil spills. Scientists and experts often disagree on which method is the best.

Lesson Review

Now that you have completed Lessons 29 and 30, focused on marine pollution, complete the chart below. Use your textbook, workbook, and class notes to help you fill in the answers.

Question	Answer
What is marine pollution (in your own words)?	

Question	Answer
What are some facts or statistics you have learned about marine pollution that have grabbed your attention?	
What is one specific problem related to marine pollution?	
Why do you think this is such a big problem?	
How is this problem caused?	
What effects does this problem have on marine animals?	

Question	Answer
How does this problem affect humans?	
What do you predict might happen if this problem is not addressed?	
What can you do to help solve this problem? What are some changes you can make to help address the issue?	

31 Humans and Coastlines

BIGIDEAS

- Wetlands are coastal environments that serve many important functions such as filtering pollutants and providing habitats for organisms.

- The environments along coastlines undergo changes that affect humans and other living things.

- Humans have had a significant impact on coastlines and wetland ecosystems.

Engage

Activate Prior Knowledge

In this Lesson, you will learn about ways in which coastlines can change and how these changes affect humans and other organisms. Use the chart below to record what you already know about these topics. After you complete the Lesson, use the chart to record new information you learned.

Before reading and trying the activities in your textbook, think about the Questions below. Record what you know about each topic in the What I Know column of the chart.

Question	What I Know	What I Learned
What are wetlands?		
Why are barrier islands important to humans and other organisms?		
How do storm surges affect coastlines?		
What are the pros and cons of coastal development?		

Explore

Practice Process Skills: MAKE MODELS

The lab on Pages 610–611 of your textbook asks you to use a model to investigate the function of a wetland. Remember, a model is a visual or physical representation of something. Models can help people understand how objects or processes work.

Models are often used to show:

- An enlarged version of something tiny, such as a cell.

- A smaller version of something vast, such as the solar system.

- A version of something that cannot be directly observed, such as Earth's inner layers.

There are many kinds of models. A diagram is a two-dimensional model. Diagrams of a microscope, for example, may be used to illustrate its parts. Diagrams do not, however, show how the parts work. Three-dimensional models, or physical models, may be more useful in showing how things work. For the *Investigating a Model of Wetlands* lab, you will build a three-dimensional model. Other types of models include mathematical equations and computer simulations.

In preparation for the lab in your textbook, think about models, how they work, and their limitations. Then, answer the Questions below.

1. Suppose you want to investigate the action of ocean waves along a beach. What kind of model would you use?

   _____

2. What elements would you want to represent in the model?

   _____

3. What materials could you use to represent these elements?

   _____

4. Describe briefly a procedure you could follow to carry out the investigation.

   _____

   _____

   _____

Explain

Vocabulary Review

Complete the chart below as you read Pages 612–614 of your textbook. Write the definition of each vocabulary term in your own words. Then, write a note to yourself on how you can remember the meaning of each term. Use the chart to review key concepts after you have finished the Lesson.

Term	Definition	How I Will Remember
Wetland		
Barrier island		
Coastal development		
Storm surge		
Dredge		

Reading Strategy: SEQUENCE OF EVENTS

Page 613 of your textbook describes how barrier islands form. Events and processes such as this often happen in a certain sequence, or order. Knowing the order in which events happen can help us see more clearly and understand a process and how it works.

After reading about the formation of barrier islands, use the Sequence of Events graphic organizer below to record in your own words the major stages of this process.

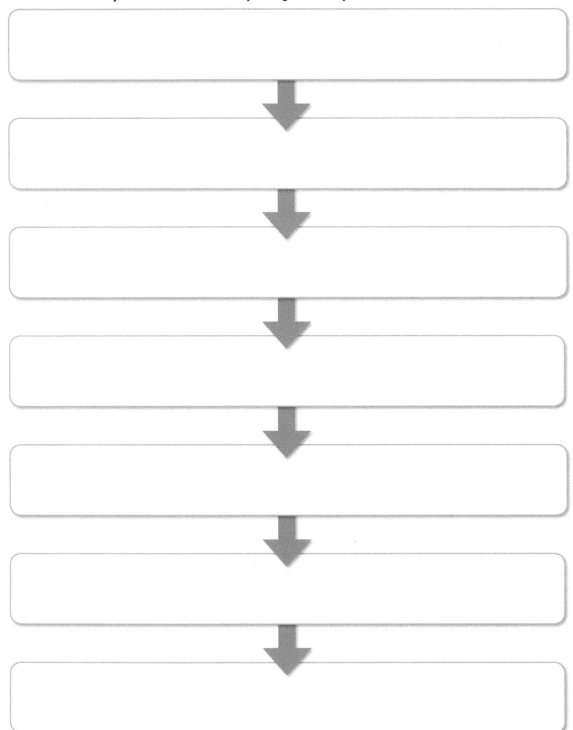

Review Key Concepts

After reading Pages 616–620 of your textbook, complete the Questions below. For Questions 1–7, fill in the blank with the correct term from the word bank.

> estuary   saltwater   bog   buffer   sediments   brackish   erosion

1. A wetland habitat where river and sea meet is an _____ .

2. The roots of wetland plants trap soil and _____ which, in turn, absorb water from a storm surge and runoff.

3. Seawalls, built to prevent _____, have adverse affects on sea turtles and other animals that nest along coastline beaches.

4. One of the many important functions of wetlands is that they serve as a _____ between the land and water.

5. Water that is a mixture of salt water and fresh water is described as _____ .

6. Mudflats and mangrove forests are two kinds of _____ wetlands.

7. A _____ is an example of a freshwater wetland.

8. What are two cause-and-effect relationships involving the development of wetlands by humans?

   _____

   _____

   _____

   _____

   _____

9. What is one way you can help to replenish wetlands?

   _____

   _____

Elaborate

Visual Literacy: Reading Maps

On Pages 621–622 of your textbook, you are asked to complete a project that involves using a contour map. A contour map is a type of topographic map. Recall from previous Lessons that topographic maps show such features as mountains, valleys, rivers, and forests, to name just a few. These features are shown on a map through the use of various lines, symbols, and colors. Contour maps show more than the location of mountains and other land features; they also show the shape, depth, and height—the contours—of these features. Contour lines show different elevations. The difference in elevation between two contour lines is called the contour interval. The contour interval changes with the terrain.

Before completing the project on Page 622 of your textbook, review how to read and interpret contour maps by answering the Questions below.

1. Look at the contour map on Page 622 of your textbook. How would you find the contour interval for this map?

   _____

2. What might you expect the contour interval of a large, very steep mountain to be compared to those shown on Page 622?

   _____

3. Look at the contour lines of the map in Figure 31.30, starting near the ocean, moving toward the map's center, and then to the upper left of the map. In your own words, describe the changes in elevation.

   _____

   _____

   _____

   _____

4. What is the highest elevation on this map?

   _____

Evaluate

Lesson Summary

- People have historically lived along coastlines because of all that coastlines have to offer.

- A model can be used to illustrate the functions of wetlands.

- Barrier islands protect coastlines from erosion and are characterized by sand dunes and wetlands.

- Barrier islands undergo constant change due to natural processes and human activities.

- Sea turtles, many other kinds of animals, and a variety of plants inhabit barrier islands and other places along a coastline.

- There are many kinds of wetlands, including freshwater and saltwater wetlands.

- Wetland habitats filter pollutants and absorb excess water from runoff and storm surge, thereby reducing flooding.

- People can prevent wetland loss through research, education, and stewardship, and by promoting conservation laws that protect marine habitats.

- Scientists make use of models to predict storm surge during hurricanes.

Lesson Review

Answer the Questions below to review the key concepts of this Lesson. Use your textbook, notes, and the previous workbook pages to help you answer the Questions.

1. In what ways are coastlines important to living things?

    _____

    _____

    _____

2. What are some functions of a wetland?

    _____

    _____

    _____

3. What natural events cause barrier islands to change?

_____

_____

_____

4. What human activities cause barrier islands to change?

_____

_____

_____

5. Do you think it is important for high school students to learn how human activities affect wetlands? Explain your reason or reasons.

_____

_____

_____

6. Suppose a wetland in one area is affected by human activities. How might organisms beyond the wetland area be affected?

_____

_____

_____

7. Why do meteorologists make storm surge predictions during hurricanes?

_____

_____

_____

Now that you have completed Lesson 31, return to the chart on Page 345 of this workbook. Using the knowledge you have gained over the course of this Lesson, reread the Questions and complete the What I Learned section of the chart.

32   The Ocean's Resources

BIGIDEAS

- The ocean is made up of both renewable and nonrenewable resources.

- Fish are typically considered a renewable resource. However due to overfishing, fish of many species are being depleted at a rate that is nonrenewable.

- Humans must work to develop solutions to ensure that the ocean's resources remain unharmed.

Engage

On Pages 626–627 of your textbook you will consider some reasons people fish and ways in which fishing is contributing to a reduction in some fish stocks. Use the information in your textbook and your prior knowledge of these topics to complete the table below. Record two observations or facts about each type of fishing.

Observations and Facts About the Reasons for Fishing		
Sport/Recreation	Commercial Fishing	Personal Fishing

Explore

Practice Process Skills: RECORD DATA

In the activities on Pages 628–629 of your textbook, you are asked to complete a data table as part of your experiment. Remember that during scientific experiments and research we often use charts and tables to record observations. Charts and tables enable you to organize, find, and interpret information quickly. A data table is one type of chart that is frequently used. In a data table, information is arranged in labeled rows and columns.

Scientists often use data tables to:

- Record quantitative and qualitative data from a multi-step process.

- Record data for each variable or trial of an experiment.

- Record the results of an experiment and any calculations done during the investigation.

Below is an example of a data table from an experiment done by a group of students. In this experiment, students were positioned at different locations along the Hudson River. Students caught fish at each location. They recorded how many of each type of fish they caught. Then they recorded all of their data into a data table. This enabled them to see which species of fish were found at each location along the Hudson River.

HUDSON RIVER FISH CAUGHT ON OCTOBER 12, 2006

| Type of Fish | \multicolumn{11}{c|}{Hudson River Mile} | Totals |
	14	18	25	28	41	61	85	97	102	115	124	
Spottail Shiner			1			1	6	23	2	11		44
Atlantic Silverside	1	5	87	21	1							115
White Perch	1	3	13		3	5	1	3		8	3	40
Striped Bass		1	15		17	6	1	3	8	1	1	53
Pumpkinseed						1	29		1	2		33
Smallmouth Bass						2	1					3
Tesselated Darter							1	1	2	10		14

Credit: New York Department of Environmental Conservation

Use the data table from the previous page to answer the following Questions.

1. Which two species were caught in the greatest number of locations?

    _____

2. As the mile marker number gets larger, the water changes from salt water to fresh water. Which species of fish seems to prefer salt water over fresh water?

    _____

Create your own data table in the space below using the following information:

Students measured the number of fish of a variety of species caught over three years in the Hudson River. The data below are what they collected:

Spottail Shiner: 2005, 6; 2006, 4; 2007, 8   Atlantic Silverside: 2005, 44; 2006, 52; 2007, 60
White Perch: 2005, 9; 2006, 5; 2007, 1   Striped Bass: 2005, 12; 2006, 4; 2007, 7
Pumpkinseed: 2005, 3; 2006, 1; 2007, 1   Smallmouth Bass: 2005, 1; 2006, 1; 2007, 1
Tessellated Darter: 2005, 3; 2006, 8; 2007, 5

Type of Fish Caught	Year		

What are two observations you can make about the information in the table?

1. _____

2. _____

Vocabulary Review

As you read Pages 630–640 of your textbook, define each vocabulary term in your own words. Then, draw a picture or write yourself a note that will help you remember each term. When you are finished, highlight fishing methods and tools used by subsistence fishers in one color. Highlight methods and tools used by commercial fisheries in another color.

Term	Definition	How I Will Remember
Subsistence fishers	Other than sport fishing primarily to feed tem	
Troll fishing	to fish w/ many lines dring be hind the boat	
Harpoon	to shoot fish w/ harpoon gun	
Commercial fisheries	bwisnesses that get money off of fishing evry day jobs	
Longlines	commercial fishing technique uses a long line calle the main line	
Trawling	Simmular to troll fishing	

Term	Definition	How I Will Remember
Gillnet	wall of net hung from a collum in the water that fish get caught on	
Purse seine fishing	a large wall of netting deployed around an entire area of school of fish	
Blast fishing	using explosives to stan or kill fish	
Overfishing	fishing to much to where the fish cant reproduce	
Bycatch	accidentally catch other fish w/ the intent to catch another specie	
Sustainable fishing	harvest fishing to basically breed fish	
Fossil fuels	a natural fuel such as coal or gas formed geologically	
Offshore drilling	drilling for oil in the ocean deep water horizon	

Reading Strategy: CAUSE and EFFECT

A fishbone diagram is a type of graphic organizer used to explore causes of a complex event or effect. Remember, a cause is the reason something happens. The effect is what happens as a result. Each "bone" on a fishbone diagram represents one of the causes that has led to an event. Using the fishbone diagram below, we will explore the fishing tools and methods used by commercial fisheries (the causes) that have led to overfishing (the effect).

> Fishbone diagrams help organize thoughts and ideas in a simple and visual way.

Using Pages 633–634 of your textbook, record on each "bone" of the fishbone diagram a fishing method that has contributed to overfishing. On the lines attached to each bone, give a brief description of the method and state how it has led to overfishing.

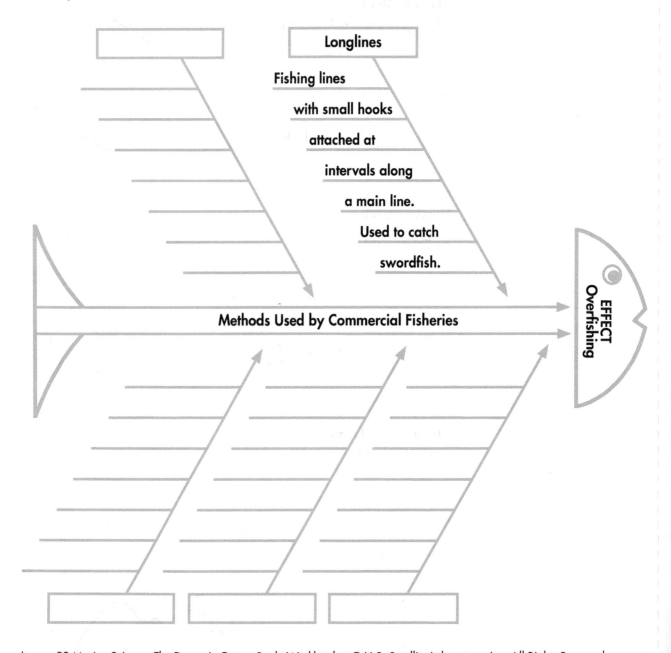

Reading Strategy: PROBLEM and SOLUTION

On Pages 634–638 of your textbook, you are reading about the problem of overfishing and how overfishing is depleting the populations of many fish and marine mammals. You are also reading about some solutions to this problem. Remember, a problem is something that needs to be fixed. A solution is a way of fixing or solving a problem.

After reading Pages 634–638 of your textbook, use the Problem and Solution graphic organizer below to record problems that lead to overfishing and the solutions to those problems. At the end of the Lesson, use the graphic organizer to review key concepts.

PROBLEM	SOLUTION
Fishermen were allowed to catch as much as their boats could carry. Certain populations of fish and shellfish were becoming overfished.	Quota laws were put into place regulating how much of a particular species fishermen can take each day, usually based on a specific number of pounds.
	Fishing seasons were put into place to ensure that organisms are not being caught during their reproductive seasons.
Sea turtles and other animals were getting caught on the J-hooks attached to longlines.	
	Turtle Excluder Devices (or TEDs) were created. A series of bars located inside the net allow larger species of fish and marine animals to pass through a flap in the net.
Seabirds, such as albatross, were diving down to get bait off hooks and were caught or entangled in longlines.	
	Minimum size limits were put into place for fish and shellfish to ensure that only adults are caught.

Evaluate

Lesson Summary

- The ocean is made up of both renewable and nonrenewable resources.

- Fish are one renewable resource. However, due to overfishing, fish of many species are being depleted at a rate that is nonrenewable.

- People who fish for food or recreation generally use methods that are sustainable.

- Nonsustainable fishing methods, used mostly by commercial industries, deplete fish populations to a point where they cannot regenerate quickly enough.

- Oil and gas are nonrenewable resources that are available in limited quantities.

- The "Tragedy of the Commons" states that humans want to use available resources, but do not want to be held responsible for their upkeep.

- We need to develop solutions to make sure that the ocean's resources remain available and intact for future generations.

Organize Your Thoughts

In the Evaluate section of your textbook, you are asked to write a letter to a government official or to create a poster informing others about a particular issue. Once you have chosen which task you will do, use the chart below to help you organize your thoughts before you write your letter, or create your poster.

Question	Answer
What is a problem you read about that you would like to think about or know more about?	
Why did you choose this issue? How does the issue make you feel?	

Question	Answer
Why is this problem occurring? State the main causes of this problem.	
Who is mainly responsible for this problem?	
What, if anything, has been done to address this problem?	
What do you think should be done to address this problem further?	
How can you or others help fix this problem?	

Now use your responses in the chart as an outline to help guide you in your letter writing, or poster creation. Good luck!

Lesson Review

In Lesson 32 you learned about subsistence and commercial fishing. Use the text and your knowledge of the topics to help you complete the Venn diagram below as a way of reviewing key topics from the Lesson. List four to five facts about each kind of fishing that are unique, as well as at least two similarities that they have.

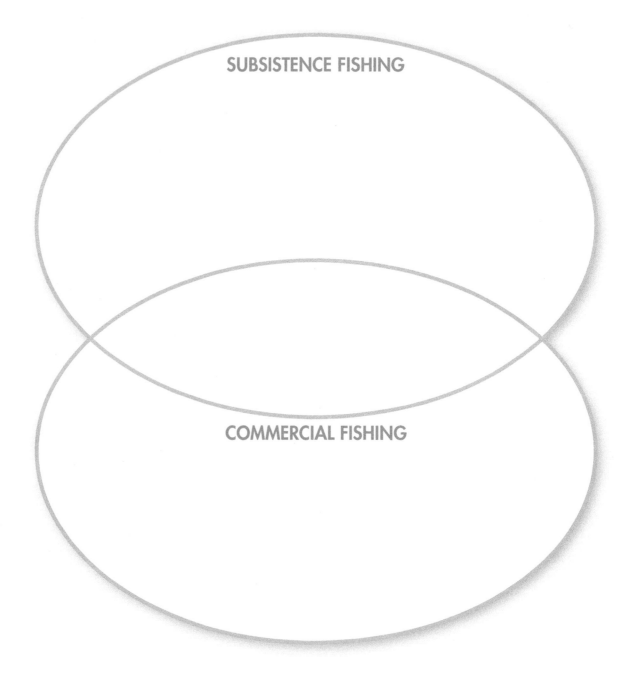

SUBSISTENCE FISHING

COMMERCIAL FISHING

33 Changing Climate

BIGIDEAS

- Earth's climate is going through a warming period.

- Climate change impacts marine organisms and ecosystems and patterns of winds and water.

Engage

Activate Prior Knowledge

In this Lesson you will learn how the ocean and the life it supports are affected by changes in climate. Use the chart below to record what you already know about these topics. After you complete the Lesson, use the chart to record new information you learned.

Before reading and trying the activities in your textbook, think about the Questions below. Record what you know about each topic in the What I Know column of the chart.

Question	What I Know	What I Learned
What is climate change?		
Why are coral reefs important?		
What effect do greenhouse gases have on our atmosphere?		
What is El Niño?		

Visual Literacy: Reading Graphs

Pages 647–649 of your textbook show several line graphs about climate change. Remember that graphs show data in a visual way and make it easier for us to see and interpret information. Being able to read and understand graphs is an important skill.

Examine the line graph below from Page 647 of your textbook and answer the Questions that follow.

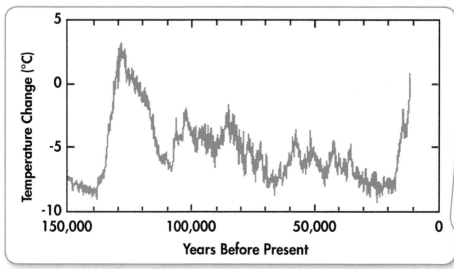

Remember from previous Lessons that a line graph is used to examine the relationship between two pieces of related data, or variables.

Credit: Petit, et al., 1999

1. What does this graph show? Use the labels to help you.

   _____

2. What information is shown along the x-axis? Recall that the x-axis is the horizontal axis.

   _____

3. What information is shown along the y-axis? Recall that the y-axis is the vertical axis.

   _____

4. What happened to the temperature between 140,000 and 130,000 years ago?

   _____

5. How did temperature change from about 100,000 years ago to about 20,000 years ago?

   _____

6. What is currently happening to the temperature on Earth?

   _____

Name Class Date

Explore

Vocabulary Review

Complete the chart below as you read Pages 650–656 of your textbook. Write the definition of each vocabulary term in your own words. Then, write a note to yourself on how you can remember the meaning of each term. Use the chart to review key concepts after you have finished the Lesson.

Term	Definition	How I Will remember
Anomaly		
Zooxanthellae		
Range of tolerance		
Coral bleaching		
Computer model		

In this Lesson you are reading about how climate change can affect certain species.

Below is a graphic organizer called a 5 W's and an H Chart. On this chart you will answer the Questions, Who, What, Where, When, Why, and How, filling in information about the effect of climate change on coral reefs. Use pages in your textbook from throughout the Lesson to help you complete the activity.

Climate Change and Coral Reefs	
What are coral reefs?	
Where are they found?	
Who lives there? (what species)	
How do they form? How old are most coral reefs today? How long do they take to grow?	
When do coral reefs become stressed?	
What happens when reefs are exposed to conditions beyond their range of tolerance?	
Why are coral reefs such a valuable resource?	

Explain

Vocabulary Review

Complete the chart below as you read Pages 656–664 of your textbook. Write the definition of each vocabulary term in your own words. Then, write a note to yourself on how you can remember the meaning of each term. Use the chart to review key concepts after you have finished the Lesson.

Term	Definition	How I Will Remember
Global climate change		
Anthropogenic		
Sea ice		
Glacial ice		
Thermal expansion		
Meltwater		

Reading Strategy: CAUSE and EFFECT

Pages 658–661 of your textbook describe some of the ideas scientists have about the causes of climate change. They also discuss some effects of climate change. Remember, a cause is the reason something happens. The effect is what happens as a result. Climate change is both an effect of human and natural activities, and a cause of other changes.

After reading Pages 658–661 of your textbook, record possible human-made causes of climate change in the first set of circles. Then, record the effects of climate change in the second set of circles.

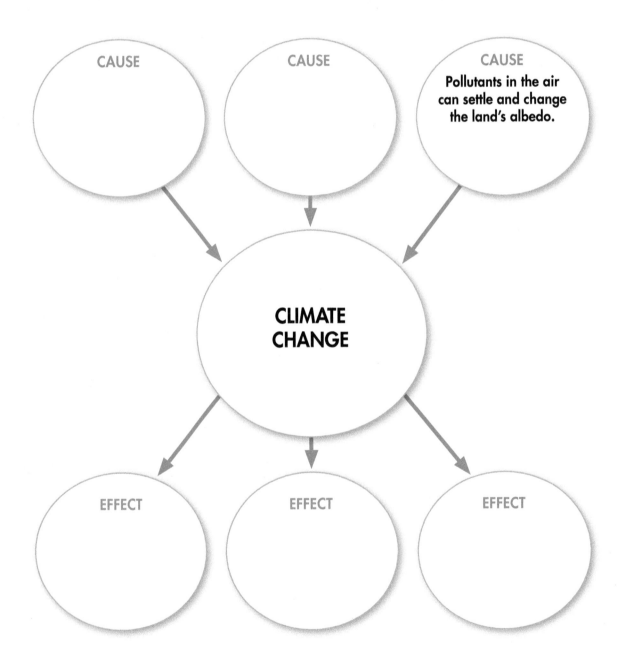

CAUSE

CAUSE

CAUSE
Pollutants in the air can settle and change the land's albedo.

CLIMATE CHANGE

EFFECT

EFFECT

EFFECT

Review What You Learned

After completing the lab on Pages 662–663 of your textbook, answer the Questions below to review what you learned.

1. What does the ice in the two beakers represent?

    _____

    _____

2. What did you predict would happen when you melted the ice in both beakers?

    _____

    _____

3. What did you observe from the *Investigating Sea Level Rise* experiment?

    _____

    _____

4. How does your prediction compare with your observations of the experiment?

    _____

    _____

    _____

5. How has your understanding of sea level changed after conducting the *Investigating Sea Level Rise* lab?

    _____

    _____

    _____

Reflect on Your Reading

Page 665 of your textbook explains that the ocean absorbs excess carbon dioxide from the atmosphere. Some feel that the ocean can readily absorb extra carbon dioxide without great cause for concern. Some believe that this process could be harmful to the ocean and marine organisms.

Use the Pros and Cons scale to record benefits and problems related to relying on the ocean to absorb excess carbon dioxide. Then, write a short paragraph explaining your position on this issue.

The Issue:

Pros	Cons

_____

_____

_____

_____

_____

_____

_____

Elaborate

Review What You Learned

After reading Pages 669–673 of your textbook, answer the Questions below to review what you learned.

1. In your own words, explain what El Niño is. _____

   _____

   _____

   _____

   _____

2. What are some examples of changes in weather that could be attributed to El Niño? Complete the concept map to demonstrate an understanding of the effects of El Niño.

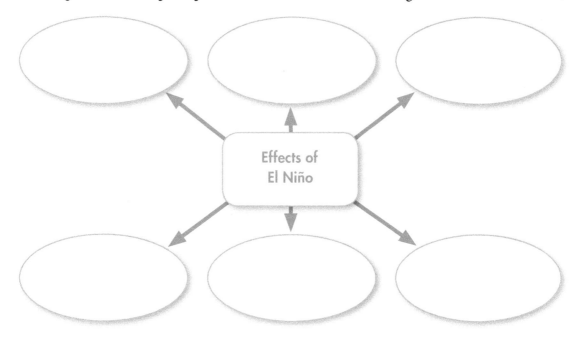

Effects of El Niño

3. Predict how marine animals might be affected by an El Niño event. _____

   _____

   _____

   _____

   _____

Evaluate

Lesson Summary

- Coral reefs support large and diverse ecosystems and can be adversely affected by changes in water temperature and carbon levels.

- Scientists disagree on the causes of global climate change, but most believe that humans have had a detrimental impact due to greenhouse gas emissions.

- Melting freshwater glaciers cause thermal expansion, warmer meltwater, and ultimately, a rise in sea level.

- Increased carbon dioxide in the atmosphere is absorbed by the ocean. This causes ocean water to have a higher acidity and makes it difficult for some organisms to build shells.

- El Niño is a phenomenon characterized by reversed winds in the tropical Pacific Ocean. It impacts weather patterns across the globe.

Review the Topic

Now that you have completed the Lesson, return to Page 363 in the workbook and complete the What I Learned column with facts you have learned during your reading, through labs, and in classroom discussions.

Organize Your Thoughts

You are asked to prepare a poster, digital presentation, or speech about global climate change in the Evaluate section of your textbook. Use the chart below to organize your thoughts before creating the presentation.

Questions	Evidence
What are three pieces of evidence that Earth is warming?	
What are three natural or human-made causes of climate change?	
What are two predicted effects of climate change?	
How could marine organisms be affected?	

34 Protecting Marine Habitats

BIGIDEAS

- Ocean literacy means understanding our influence on the ocean and the ocean's influence on us. Developing ocean literacy is an important step in learning how to protect our ocean resources.

- The creation of marine protected areas (MPAs) is one way we can conserve ocean resources.

- International cooperation is a necessary part of preserving renewable resources.

Engage

Lesson Warm Up

In this Lesson, you will learn about ocean literacy and ways to protect our ocean resources. Using Page 678 of your textbook and your knowledge of these topics, explore ocean literacy with the concept map below.

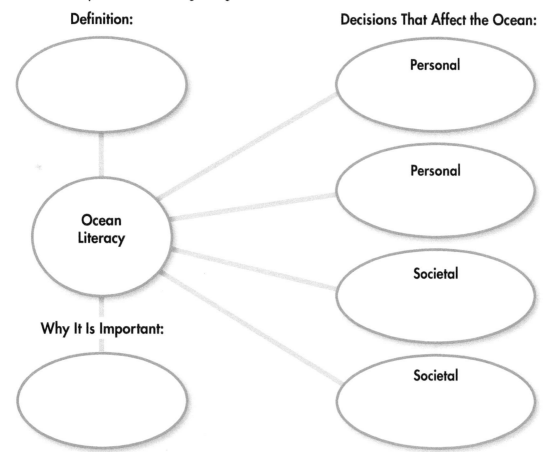

Definition:

Decisions That Affect the Ocean:

Ocean Literacy

Personal

Personal

Societal

Why It Is Important:

Societal

Explore

Review What You Learned

After reading the text and completing the Cyberlab on Pages 680–682 of your textbook, answer the Questions below to review what you learned.

1. Describe Hawaii's landscape and ecosystems in your own words. _____

   _____

   _____

2. Name at least four animals that live in and around the Hawaiian marine protected areas

   (MPAs). _____

   _____

   _____

3. What species did your group choose to track? In what year did you first observe data for

   these species? Where did your animals travel during the first year you chose? Did the

   travel patterns for these species change from one year to another? If yes, how? _____

   _____

   _____

   _____

4. How did the travel patterns of these animals relate to the location of the Hawaiian MPAs?

   Do the animals stay close to or within the MPAs? Explain. _____

   _____

   _____

5. What else would you like to learn about these species and MPAs? Record at least two new

   questions you have. _____

   _____

   _____

Explain

Reading Strategy: SEQUENCE OF EVENTS

The Explain section of your textbook discusses some steps that have been taken over time to preserve our ocean resources. Recording these events on a timeline is a useful way to review and remember what you read. Remember, a timeline is a visual guide that helps you see a sequence of historical events. Timelines can help you understand how things happened or changed over time and can help you make connections between events.

After reading Pages 681–686 of your textbook, record the events related to marine protection in the correct order on the timeline. An example has been done for you.

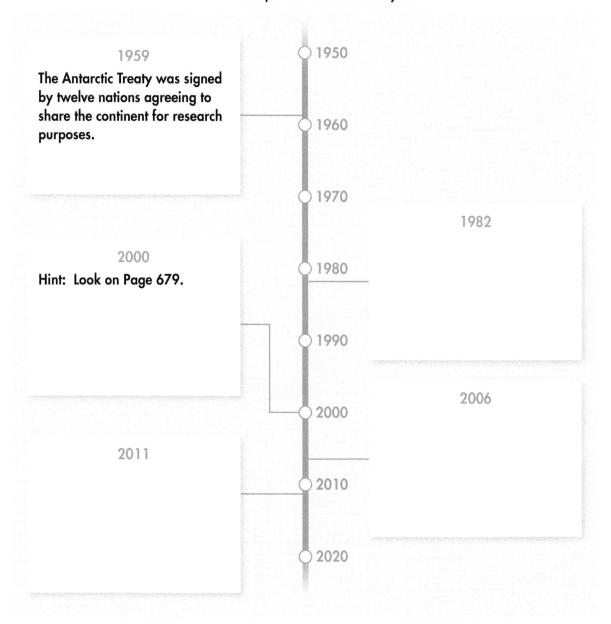

1959
The Antarctic Treaty was signed by twelve nations agreeing to share the continent for research purposes.

2000
Hint: Look on Page 679.

2011

1950

1960

1970

1980

1982

1990

2000

2006

2010

2020

Review What You Learned

After reading Pages 684–686 of your textbook, answer the Questions below to review what you learned.

1. What are Regional Fisheries Management Organizations (RFMOs)? Describe some goals of these organizations. _____

   _____

   _____

   _____

2. Describe the continent of Antarctica. _____

   _____

   _____

   _____

3. Why does Antarctica have a long history of international cooperation? _____

   _____

   _____

   _____

4. What were the three major decisions that came out of the Antarctic Treaty? _____

   _____

   _____

   _____

5. List at least three of the problems that organizations and preservationists face in

   Antarctica. _____

   _____

   _____

   _____

Complete the graphic organizer below with information about two types of MPAs.

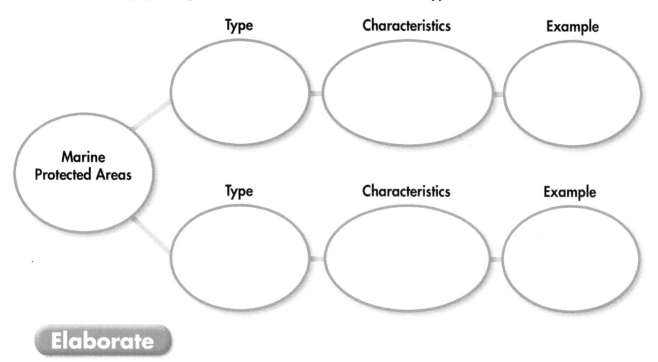

Type   Characteristics   Example

Marine Protected Areas

Type   Characteristics   Example

Elaborate

Build Background

The Elaborate section of your textbook asks you to research animals and conditions of one of Earth's Polar Regions. Your ultimate goal is to design an MPA for this region.

Before answering the Questions in your textbook, build background knowledge about your assigned region by completing the chart below.

Research Question	Answer
What are some characteristics of your region?	
What is the weather and climate like? How do they change throughout the year?	
What is the environment like? How does it change throughout the year?	

Research Question	Answer
What organisms live in your region?	
What adaptations enable these organisms to live in this environment?	
What do these organisms eat? How would a food web diagram of the ecosystem look?	
What are some behaviors of these animals? Do any of them migrate? If so, where do they go?	
Aside from seasonal changes, how else are these regions changing?	

Evaluate

Lesson Summary

- Ocean literacy means understanding the ocean's value to life on Earth and our impact on the ocean.

- Knowing how we affect the ocean enables us to make responsible decisions related to our use of the ocean and marine protection.

- The creation of marine protected areas (MPAs) is helping to ensure that marine ecosystems are protected. National Marine Sanctuaries and National Marine Monuments are two types of MPAs created by the United States.

- Exclusive Economic Zones (EEZs) give countries the rights to waters within 200 miles of their own coastlines. Within these boundaries, a country can make its own decisions regarding how to use and regulate these waters.

- It is still difficult to regulate international waters, because no one country owns them. Regulation requires the cooperation and agreement of many nations.

- Several organizations have been formed to try to encourage sustainable fishing practices and responsible actions in international waters. Following these rules is voluntary and cannot be enforced.

- We need to cooperate internationally to develop ways to preserve marine habitats and the organisms that rely on the ocean.

Organize Your Thoughts

At the end of this Lesson, you are asked to design an MPA and prepare a poster and presentation describing the MPA. Use the chart on the next page to help you organize your thoughts and arrange your information as you work on this project.

Research Question	Answer
Where are you creating your MPA?	
Why have you chosen this area?	
What species will you be protecting?	
Why is an MPA needed in this area to protect these species?	
What nations will be involved in the creation of this MPA?	
What rules are you creating for this MPA? What is the reasoning behind these rules?	
How can you convince national and international decision makers that your rules are essential and will be effective?	
What scientific data (animal tracking, sea ice imagery, etc.) can you include on your poster to support your ideas?	

Lesson Review

Throughout the Lessons in this textbook, you learned about the ocean, its organisms, and the need to protect our marine resources. These Lessons have helped to build your ocean literacy. To review what you learned, write a persuasive letter about the importance of ocean literacy. In a persuasive letter the writer tries to convince a person, or group of people, to see things in a certain way or to act in a way the writer is suggesting.

A persuasive letter often has this format:

The 1st paragraph: Should be short (2 to 4 sentences); tells your audience who you are and why you are writing to them; introduces the topic or issue; often includes a fact or statistic to grab the audience's attention.

The 2nd paragraph: Talks about some of the facts related to the topic or issue.

The 3rd paragraph: Tells why you think the issue is important; gives specific suggestions of what the audience can do to address the problem.

The closing paragraph: Should be short (2 to 4 sentences); summarizes your viewpoint and restates what you think; reiterates what you are hoping they will do; thanks them for their time. Don't forget to sign your letter.

Use the information you learned from the textbook, the website, and the DVD to convince your audience that ocean literacy is critical to preserving our ocean.

_____ (date)

_____ (opening)

_____

_____

_____

_____

_____

_____

_____

_____

_____

_____

_____

_____

_____ (closing)

_____ (signature)